THE SELF-ESTEEM MAP

Martin Ross

INTRODUCTION.

On a train trip I bought a set of children's water colors. It was being sold by one of the thousands of foot peddlers. It came with a small thin brush on a plastic tray.

I felt trapped in a life that I did not choose.

I was very uncomfortable with my past, with my personality, with the decisions I had made in my life ... with my mind, with the way I had turned up and a lot more. And I said:

- Maybe I can distract myself by drawing something.

And since then, on some evenings I would retire to a corner with a bowl of water, few pages to paint on, a black pencil and the set of water colors. Until that day, I had never painted.

Some, perhaps, might think that I should not be pursuing such interest. I do not care because I enjoy it.

Anyway, this did not help me get out of the well. It entertained me a little for a short while, but not enough.

I was still weighed down by the bag of contempt for my own person.

I still suffered from an acute lack of self-love that turned me into a disheartened soul who had given up completely, to be carried away by the stream of life.

I had experienced these moods very early in life.

At times I would fall asleep on bed entangled with depression. It was not the first time that discouragement took control of my soul and made me lose taste for life.

But this time it was much stronger. I felt worse than ever. It appeared to me as something inevitable, definitive and unquestionable.

I did not want to leave the house. I did not want to get dressed. I did not want to wake up at logical hours. I did not want to attend to my work as needed, nor did I want to play any sport. Neither did I want to go out with friends or women. I did not want to strive to be any better.

Nothing interested me. There was no plan or expectation from the future that I could wake up to with enthusiasm.

I dedicated myself to painting with the watercolors and listening to music. I showed my paintings to some friends and they said that I lacked technique. Yet I enjoyed it.

Then I began to jot down some notes in a notebook with green cover and whose leaves had black lines and red margins.

The issue of self-esteem attracted my attention.

Self esteem was just the tip of the iceberg, I continued to write on vanity, on social prestige, charismatic personalities, seduction and relationships between man and woman. I also wrote on the importance of vanity in the world today. A

world as vain as never before and how this vain
and exaggerated world pushes us towards the
destruction of our self-esteem.

And envy? The ease with which envy maddens
us without our noticing anything.

I wrote about admiration as the fuel for
infatuation. Social ties, charisma. Personality
and character formation.

Subjects that I had always been curious
about, but which to me seemed different now.

What I'm presenting here is a summation of
my reflections.

More than reflections, "The Self-Esteem Map"
is one of the most powerful tools you might have
seen which would help you explore or roam around
the realm of the human soul and learn some
practical tips that can help you transform your
everyday life. Anyway, I am going to experiment
with your feelings, by asking you many questions.
After reading the book, you will get to know of
many aspects about yourself that were hitherto
unknown even to you.

I think it is a new perspective with which
to see the world, to view our own feelings ... A
way to know a little more about ourselves.

So, from time to time, I'll ask you
questions. Questions about your fears, about your
self-esteem, about how you approach life, about
your parents, your relationships, your style of
seduction, your methods to achieve your dreams,
your childhood, your character ... and your life
partner.

It is important that you spend time meditating upon these questions, and that you answer them sincerely because this is how we would get to know of our similarities and differences.

You will see that this book is presented like a session where the writer is the patient and the reader is the doctor. There is a bit of dramatization in these two roles, as in many things that you will read and which relate to me in reality.

There is some fiction, but it is only to make it easy for me to explain all my ideas, and to enable us to go on checking if they really do describe what we are.

In other words, take enough time to answer honestly and carefully the questions put to you; because there we'll get to see what we are like. Sometimes if I sound too naive or say weird things, I ask for some understanding. I'm as normal a person as anyone else. Many a times I am just a mendicant of affection, or like a child craving so much for attention from others that I act funny just to be noticed.

I'm too stunned and scared by the stereotypes and try to change or rebel or try and be different just to save myself from these deceptions; to protect myself from everything. But with a little understanding, you will realize that we are very similar, because we are all very similar and yet very different.

This book is presented in the form of a diary with some dramatics. There is a bit of fantasy. But the important thing is that it searches for the sincerity of the soul. Only honesty can help us find ourselves.

Only if we are sincere and attentive can we discover the special way in which we live out our vanity. And thanks to that we manage to be a little less enslaved by it and even turn it into a tool to improve our lives. You might say that these are nothing but ramblings of a madman who bought some watercolors and began to philosophies out of the blue. And yes, it's true. But it was a pretty way to fight the darkness that had invaded me.

-I-

Now I am going to tell you many things. I
need to bring it all out.

And at the same time I am going to suggest
to you a way to understand many of these very
things. If all goes well, this is also going to
help you use me like a mirror in order to discover
many things about yourself.

Come on! Let us together help each other!

I suggest to you an exercise to make things
simpler: we are going to imagine that you are my
doctor, my psychologist.

Let us imagine that I enter your office,
make myself comfortable on your divan & my words
begin to fill the air.

It does not matter if you have not studied
psychology nor if you are into the oriental
methods of meditation, or such things which are
seen in these texts.

What is important is that you be curious to
get to know the soul of a fellow human that
reflects his self esteem.

I want to recount to you a bit about my
moods that led me to reflect on these things. Be a
bit patient please because we have a long chat
about ourselves ahead

-1-

I suffer. I ask myself this question: And
why do I suffer?

And I come to a conclusion: I suffer because
I despise myself.

Rather, I suffer for real things in my life,
for memories, for faults, for things that are
happening to me, things that lead me to despise
myself, "contempt" is the right word.

And when I despise myself I lose the desire
to leave the house, I lose the desire to get
dressed, I lose the desire to get out of bed, to
bathe, to brush my teeth, to clean the room, to
fight, to live.

And discouragement overcomes me. It's
terrible.

-2-

Now that I set out to look at this from the
outside, even if it's funny, it amazes me. Isn't
life too mysterious and beautiful for a person to
suffer a lot just because he demeans himself?

Many times this is said out there as a
rumor: that everyone has a bad time, that they
want the luck of the other, that they set
unattainable goals for their own happiness. But I
am intrigued by the unbreakable relationship
between "disgust at oneself" and "suffering."

Can't a person say, *"Okay, I'm a mess, but
I'm going to have fun and have a good time
anyway"*?

-3-

I wonder:

Why is this so? What is behind that?

At first glance it always seemed to me to be
useless reasoning, but, after thinking about it a
few times, as I was saying, I came to an answer
that calls my attention: I suffer because I deeply
despise myself.

-4-

I ask myself these two questions:

And why do I despise myself? And how can I
stop despising myself?

I am sure that the contempt I have for
myself is the source from which this thick black
water springs that floods my whole soul and my
life. Contempt is the reason that I spend hours
and hours lying on the bed and that the room has a
zoo of buns of clothes thrown everywhere, bus
tickets, unwashed sheets, packages of cookies and
papers written anywhere. side.

But ... And what does it rely on? What was
it that led me to despise myself?

-5-

The first answer is that it leans "on
something."

The first answer is that it leans "on
something."

Even if I want to, I can't say: "I accept
myself as I am!" as my colleagues -the smarties at
the bars- advise me... I can't.

-6-

The smarties at the bars

Later we will talk about important things that are talked about in bars:

About how we are. On our personality, the charismatic personalities, and on the enigmas of seduction ...

I promise later!

I promise you that I am going to tell you very practical things about the forces of seduction, about your own personality, about your way of reaching your goals, about your own style ...

I am going to tell you things that you have never seen before and that were always there.

Like everyone ... this patient also goes into the gardens of the soul with practical interests. So, for you to be interested in this journey through these mazes, it is good that you know what my interests are and what things I want to talk to you about.

And I am sincere if I tell you that the way to grow and to form the personality, the charisma, the emotional magnetism, how the different peoples are (how rare we are!) And, above all, the soft follies of seduction ... are my best interests.

What happens to men with some women?

We know them, we talk to them for a while, from time to time we cross them, we don't give them importance, maybe we belittled them, and suddenly they did "something" that caught us. What did that crazy woman do? How did it catch us?

Because of cultural impositions, because of something strange that happens, because of "something", we are no longer as men as before.

There are no men. I don't know what happened, later we will talk about it, but we are no longer so men. Now we are afraid.

We spend time with a woman, a few months, maybe a year, and suddenly I don't remember: nothing matters, we just have to escape.

What happened? How many times did that happen to us? Why do we get so entangled in these hypocritical relationships, with an expiration date ... with an expiration date that we set for ourselves? And didn't any sincere mirror ever tell us that we are chronic, lying, and very afraid of compromise?

I'm getting a lot ahead of myself, but the subject of the soft follies that are unleashed with seduction is one of the subjects that interests me most.

Much about you I can say on this matter.

Many things about your personality, your childhood, the way you fight for your projects, your self-esteem, the special way that your style gives the art of seduction.

Maybe ... the two of us ... doctor and patient, we are similar to the alchemists of before.

The alchemists were looking for the philosopher's stone which was what would allow them to build the gold of the earth. They were the first chemists. And I think chemistry had, at the time, the same evolution that psychology has today, sociology. Or the science of seducing, the branch of social science that is without a doubt the most important of all. Alchemists were confident… confident in the power of knowledge.

The two of us, who have ventured into the dark and enigmatic forests of the human soul believing that we are going to find important and practical things are two optimists as well.

The problem is that, in order for me to tell you about the practical things that interest us the most, it is first very important and necessary that you familiarize yourself with these basic pillars of the "Map of Self-Esteem", the theory that I want to show you.

I am sure that if you put in the effort needed to incorporate them... you will feel the change in your blood. Because ideas are to life what blood is to the body & in this way we will become similar. And when you understand, when you understand well what it is all about, you will be able to have a meaningful conversation with me which will help you see things that you ignore now... things that are going to influence you & that are going to change you.

One of these things -I am trying to resist the temptation of moving on to one of my main interests- is falling in love... understood to be a kind of gentle madness... What is your special style of seduction?

I can't wait for us to talk about more practical and much more interesting things. But to be able to do it with the depth that these topics require, it is important that I continue presenting you these basic notions.

… It is essential that we continue with this exercise of recreation of the moments that led me to the elaboration of the theory that I want to present to you.

Then let's not go ahead, and let's continue

-7-

Let's keep going:

And why do I despise myself? Why do I have a very bad opinion of myself?

Looking at it several times I find specific answers to these questions. It is concrete things - things that can be pointed out - that are behind the deep contempt I have for myself.

I mean that it is "real data" that leads me to have a very bad opinion of me.

They are features of me or memories of things I did, memories that come to visit me at night and lead me to hate myself.

Many times I say "I wish I had not done this" or also "I would have liked to do things differently" and that is useless and much less to get out of this boredom, this inertia, this loss of desire to live.

I also think of some flaws of mine. And they are the ones that lead me to have a horrible opinion of myself that later won't let me get out of bed. Neither do I go out and live life. For example, I think about my physical appearance:

That I look too skinny, too short, too sad. I
think of the tone of my voice that I hear weak,
trembling, almost pleading.

Or I think of my work as being very
changeable, and sometimes I work and sometimes I
don't. That it is a job that does not allow me to
develop personally as I would like and that does
not "produce anything" (I am going to tell you),
or I think about the way people see me… which also
seems sad to me, or my studies.

I meditate on these defeats and shames, over
and over, like a hypnotist.

-8-

Now, the time has come to start presenting
you with the theory I was building with my own
depression (don't laugh… I know you laughed, I saw
you).

Listen well:

I am going to call these horrible "data from
my real life": "anti-feats". And on the other
hand: the "real data" that help me improve my
opinion of me: "feats".

All those things you respect about people
are "feats." All that which make you belittle a
person are "anti-feats."

For example, if you respect a person who
came out of an adverse environment and was able to
succeed in life and indulge himself, you respect
him for his feat of success. Another example would
be: if you despise a thief, you despise him
because he "steals", robberies are "anti-feats",
which lead you to despise him.

Another example: if you respect an acquaintance of yours a lot because he helps the poor a lot and does good works ... then your respect is based on "the feats" that are his good works. Other: If you respect a guy for his career and for everything he strives to do, your respect is based on the feat of his work.

-9-

In order for you to understand me, I suggest that you try to notice what things come to your mind when you suffer from a lack of self-esteem ...

I mean: when inside your head there are voices that criticize you a lot, that challenge you, that criticize you with cruelty ...

What do they tell you?

Do they tell you you're selfish? Do they tell you you're lazy? Do they tell you that your salary is low?

What do the inner voices tell you when you are at the hell? How do they insult you? How do they punish you?

… All those arguments that the voice of "self-criticism" uses when you fall into the wells of your Self-Esteem, are what I am calling anti-feats.

They are always "real data" that speak of your own life, of the situation of your own life. They are "real data" that make you feel less

valuable, that you deserve less respect, that your
ego is diminished.

     You need to pay attention to them. We will
talk about many more things with respect to you
when we understand the topic of feats & anti-feats
better. Many things about your style, your life,
your personality, and your attempts at self
improvement... we will talk about many such
things.

     The feats and anti-feats are like two
psychological magnets that unleash two opposite
forces that pull you from one side to another.

     -10-

     I am going to give you a well exaggerated
example of what a "feat" is.

     At one time in my life I practiced boxing. I
really liked that sport, especially in moments of
frustration or fear I would go to the club and hit
the bag until all the bad vibes were unloaded. At
one point I took it quite seriously and was
leaving five times a week to train.

     The point is, it was never more than an
amateur sport, but I had a few fights.

     Well, let's imagine for a moment that I
become a professional boxer.

     Can you imagine me: Don't laugh back.

     Well, let's imagine that I am also good. I
train hard. I run every day. Rope, push-ups, I
start fighting with others and I start to win.
With every fight I win I feel good, I feel
"proud", and I have a reason to show off and above

all to feel confident to continue training and to
improve.

One day I fight for the national boxing
title, and I win it ... They call me to the center
of the ring and they raise my hand high, and they
leave the other's hand under.

That would be a "feat", winning the boxing
title.

At the moment I prefer not to talk to you
about more concrete and achievable "feats" that
tempt me or that I sometimes caress in dreams, but
you will already be understanding what I mean by
the word "feat" and the word "anti-feat".

-11-

The "feats" then are like "magic stones"
that you are looking for in your life because they
have the virtue of making you happy.

They give you the opportunity to "self-
value", "like" yourself. They lead you to show
off, to feel important, to feel like a person of
value.

And the "anti-feats" are like "burning
fathoms" that dodge them and that -when they reach
you- they attack you until they defeat you, and
then they become memories that look for you at
night and shout at you *look what you lived
through, now you will have to despise yourself!*.

Are you incorporating these concepts?

They are key so that you can enter the
interior journey that we are going to make.

But, although they may look "strong" or "safe" or "confident" from the outside, they behave in that way because they are extremely panicked by all kinds of "real data" that could question their " self-respect. "

An example close to me is my younger sister's husband. He is a big, tall, erect guy. When they invite me to eat at their house if we discuss politics, religion, or anything, he can never give up. Without you asking him anything, he tells you how many women he got up before being with my sister and how brave a thug he is when they put him to the test. She doesn't know the word "forgive me" and her lips are going to die virgins of the phrase "I need your help". He can never lose anything and he can never go wrong in anything.

He's talking about himself all the time!

It's easy to imagine, isn't it? Now they have gone on a trip, but when they come back, if one day I go home to eat I will tell you. I suspect she doesn't love me a bit, it's just my sister who insists that I go.

There is also one thing: one of these "Egocentric" is not only afraid of events, let us say forceful as: "that your life is a failure" or "that you are left alone" or "that you lose your job" or that "betray you the people you loved the most "but they are afraid of all kinds of" mini-failures ", even the most insignificant ones such as:" that you mismatched the tie with the shirt ", or that" you were not right in treating a so-and-so, "or that" you played tennis worse than a mengano and it was only fair that you lose. "

These "arrogant" is not that they have a "strong self-esteem" but quite the opposite. They have such a weak self-esteem that they need to take care of it all the time from any defeat or shame, no matter how small.

There are very small "anti-feats" but many times we run away from them.

Defeat in an argument, or saying: "I was wrong", or saying: "Sorry." Doesn't it strike your attention how, in everyday life, we reject the little-defeats of every day and we escape with allergies?

It looks like an obstacle course!

The issue of escaping "anti-feats" and pursuing "feats" is emotional ... we do it without realizing it!

Have you ever been with one of those men who can't admit they lost, or were wrong, or did something wrong? They are terrible!

But, although they may look "strong" or "safe" or "confident" from the outside, they behave in that way because they are extremely panicked by all kinds of "real data" that could question their " self-respect. "

An example close to me is my younger sister's husband. He is a big, tall, erect guy. When they invite me to eat at their house if we discuss politics, religion, or anything, he can never give up. Without you asking him anything, he tells you how many women he got up before being

with my sister and how brave a thug he is when
they put him to the test. She doesn't know the
word "forgive me" and her lips are going to die
virgins of the phrase "I need your help". He can
never lose anything and he can never go wrong in
anything.

He's talking about himself all the time!

It's easy to imagine, isn't it? Now they
have gone on a trip, but when they come back, if
one day I go home to eat I will tell you. I
suspect she doesn't love me a bit, it's just my
sister who insists that I go.

There is also one thing: one of these
"Egocentric" is not only afraid of events, let us
say forceful as: "that your life is a failure" or
"that you are left alone" or "that you lose your
job" or that "betray you the people you loved the
most "but they are afraid of all kinds of" mini-
failures ", even the most insignificant ones such
as:" that you mismatched the tie with the shirt ",
or that" you were not right in treating a so-and-
so, "or that" you played tennis worse than and you
lose.

These "arrogant" is not that they have a
"strong self-esteem" but quite the opposite. They
have such a weak self-esteem that they need to
take care of it all the time from any defeat or
shame, no matter how small.

-13-

Today not all "real data" breaks the opinion
that got from me.

I have been able to face some minor problems for a long time effort… I can apologize or admit that I was wrong or realize an error. But the real pain is the ladies tougher, heavier, stronger, anti-feats that have to do with life as a whole.

They are the ones who sometimes become the queens of me spirit and are present all the time inside me. They are the ones that brought me to your clinic.

-14-

I imagine you ask me:

-Can't you convince yourself that you are a great value without paying attention to anything? Can't you tell yourself "I love myself a lot and on Wednesday "? What if you look in the mirror and say "I'm a big, I'm a big, I'm a big "and voila? Can't you go up your self-esteem because you feel like it and bye?

I can even see your irritated face. But ... its impossible!

Although it calls my attention a lot, it is impossible.

I need the mysterious "feats".

I need to find "concrete things" with which to be able to establish or create a "good opinion of myself". I can say "I am great because of this, this and this" but I cannot say " I am great because I believe so...".

I need some "basis".

These "concrete things" are, for example, what make me believe that I am "unique and irreplaceable" as they say in those self-help books.

Or if not, they could be more specific things such as merits, successes, advantages, talents, sacrifices, the work... but always "something real".

I need to find "real things" to start founding or to build a "good opinion of myself".

-15-

I don't know if you're going to accompany me with this. Maybe you're in the sidewalk opposite.

Maybe you are one of those who believe that a person can say:

- I value myself for what I am, beyond everything.

I do not. We can both sit down to discuss this, but I am convinced of what I tell you: it cannot be solved like this.

At least in my case I need "concrete and certain things" to be able to build a good opinion of me.

Of course it would be a lot healthier than a person can say: *"Regardless of how I go or beyond everything, I am going to feel great admiration for myself. "*

… But that cannot be done and all Self-Esteem have - some more and some less - a degree of dependency on "Real things" in each person's life

-16-

I guess you are quickly incorporating these ideas … and without giving them enough attention to crystallize inside of you forever.

They are simple: What is the feat?

From a point of view more theoretical ... What is it? Is it the proof that our organism to recognize our genes as the strongest and capable and, therefore, the only ones worthy of passing to the next generation?

What is anti-feat? Is it proof that our body fails in the environment and therefore our genes do not do they deserve to pass to the next generation?

Are we machines made to improve and reproduce?

Why do we enjoy feats so much? Why do we escape anti-feats so much?

-17-

They are questions… questions so you can continue elaborating from these notions…. But I don't give you answers, because I don't have them. I'm only interested that these enigmatic concepts ...

There are more practical and impactful things in your life concrete that we will try to learn later if you can get familiar with these two bugs: feats and anti-feats.

I'm not going to give you an unbreakable and magical Self-esteem, and I invite you to stop reading if you have that expectation. I'm not going to give the clues to achieve the feats ... those same feats that today you caress in dreams.

... But if you pay attention to these concepts - feats and anti-feats - something is going to forever change within you and, with exercise and effort, you will be able to improve in many things .

Come on! Let us together help each other!

-18-

We need self-esteem to be happy and "real bases" to have self-esteem ... in other words we need "feats".

-19-

These days most of the things that make me happy or they give me happiness are small "feats".

I get up early, I go outside, I walk through the blocks and I buy the newspaper, and when I come back I have the breakfast that I prepared before leaving. I wear good clothes for gymnastics and I leave the house with the keys to run and then

I turn everything sweaty and I take a bath and I look like as new.

-20-

I am happy to strive and meet my goal of run, it gives me joy when my will overcomes my

laziness, I am happy to have my breakfast
prepared, I am happy to have good clothes that I
can wear later. And also of course I am very happy
with the job.

-21-

My last job does not bring me great income
but I likes: I am renting houses for cinema and
advertising.

I go to the house, I look at it, I see the
conditions of lighting and space to place the
equipment of the filming, and then, if it helps, I
make the owner sign the piece of paper and
sometimes I get a producer to see her and take
some photos that are later on file.

You have to imagine me touring production
companies with a folder in hand with my houses and
trying to convince the "Location managers" to come
see them.

It may be many days that I work without
receiving a penny in return, but when I make an
operation the truth that everything is compensated
and it is a very important "feat" for course,
because it fills me with "pride" to be able to
achieve something.

-22-

Very well!!

This is a good method to recognize the
mysterious thing called "feat": it is that what
makes you feel "proud".

If you did something -or something that
happened to you, something that you posses- that

makes you feel "proud" and you feel happy to know it and feel like letting the whole world know of it, then it is... one of those famous "feats".

Is there something in your life that you would like to show off in front of your friends? Is there something that you are proud of and that urges you to let the world know of it?

That is a feat.

Look carefully what are the most important "feats" of your life.

Pay attention: these are the things you like to tell your

 friends, the points of your life that you touch when you "You strut", when you "show off", when you feel a little tickle pleasure in the Vanity.

What are your feats?

Of what do you like to talk about when enjoying the pleasure of vanity? What do you brag about? What makes you show off?

What topics do you like to talk about when you enjoy the pleasure of Vanity? What are you strutting about? From what things presume?

What things do you boast about?

Note: we are talking about emotional issues. So not everyone can learn to discover and identify feats and anti-feats in their lives.

It is necessary, first, to have the ability to observe one's emotion, to learn to "see" all these things. And this is a difficult exercise that is not for everyone.

-23-

We better go on, come on I swear we are
going to help each other between the two:

Where do we have to look first if we want to
"see" any human group? What is the great motor
that moves the human ?

Some will say that it is "the will to
power". Others will say which is the "sexual
desire" that has strange forms when it is covered,
others will give more weight to the economic part,
and each one will have your own idea.

Is it a relentless fight for power behind
all human conflicts, even couple conflicts? Is it
eternal fight between God and the Devil, between
"temptation" and "virtue"?

Each one will have their way of seeing it,
their beliefs, their

posture, but for your patient the most decisive of
all is "the Vanity".

-24-

If you want to understand a human group what
you have to to do is to look first of all at what
are its main "feats" and "anti-feats".

When you have them identified you will be
able to know who are the "idols" and "heroes" and
who are outcasts and "anti-heroes" whom this
group looks up to or despises respectively.

That this group will despise or admire in
one case or another. You'll then see where is the
"social prestige", and, as the flies around the

sugar, you're going to see all the people perch
and hover around the main "feats" of that same
group.

You will always have "the different" who
have a strange and mysterious behavior, and you're
also going to see the "Charismatics" who are those
that this group tends to imitate a lot more than
other people, and the "seducers" and ... well I'm
overtaking too much, we're going to get to all
that more late.

I will give you an example.

In our days "being fat" is one of the main
"anti-feat" for women and, above all, for young
women. The top clothing brands do not make large
sizes to avoid burning. The idea is that if, for
example, a woman of obese dimensions buy a t-shirt
of your brand and stroll down the avenue, then the
other women when they see her pass will despise
her and not they are going to want to use nothing
of that brand that is going to be like a "fat
brand ".

With anti-feat anti-heroes are made ...

But I am rushing again; we are going to have
a better look at these point later. The idea now
is that you begin to appreciate that every group
has its peculiar "anti-feats" and "feats".
Recognizing them is very important for
understanding each group.

The better way would be looking "within
ourselves" because each one of us is always a part
of some group or the other; each one of us in a
"product of their environment".

It is important that you begin to familiarize with this perspective of looking at the world so that we can take our discussion further.

Don't forget: a "feat" is that thing that gives you pride and that makes you want to tell everyone, that makes you feel an unstoppable thirst to spread it and show it, and that, the more powerful it is, the more you like to give it to know.

You should start paying attention to these bugs.

-25-

Try to notice: What things of yours make you happy? Where are your moments of happiness of the day?

Do you boast of your beauty? Do you brag about your friendships?

Do you brag about how well you know how to treat women? Do you boast of your relationships with women? Do you brag about your sports?

Do you brag about your work? Do you boast about your husband

What are your feats?

-26-

I guess your current thinking: We do not need to undergo a test to recognize the feats and the anti-feats in our daily lives.

And yes: we already know what they are, we think obvious.

At some point in our life we have learn to recognize a feat can help us have a better self-esteem and more social prestige.

Is that at some point in our lives we learned to see what things - if we succeed - can help us to have a better self-esteem and greater prestige.

In other words: somewhere within us there is a "general record of feats" that tells us for example *"if your salary increases, your self-esteem will grow as well"*.

More than general record the right word so it would be "map".

-27-

I'm talking about a "map" that shows you in which regions -or possibilities of life- your self-respect and your social prestige will increase and in which others everything contrary.

A map that shows you your position with respect to these regions or zones. A map that shows you the direction you have than to continue to seek self-esteem.

This is the first introduction that I give you about "The Map of Self-esteem ".

The idea is not that we complicate ourselves. I am talking to you of something quite simple: a kind of general register that you have in your mind and it tells you what are the things you should achieve so that your Ego grows and so that - at the same time - you circle of people respect you and appreciate you more.

Depending on how your "Self-Esteem Map" and "your case" are, these things can be suppose you are cuter, skinnier, that you look younger, that you have a higher salary, that you are more cultured, that you do some better sport, that you are more muscular, that you are a more good person, that you are more hard-working, that you are a better father...

We are talking about a great "General record of feats" that will be somewhere in your head, which feeds all the time from what you see around yours.

-28-

The problem is that the position of a person on the "Self Steem Map" depends on things that cannot be controlled.

Sometimes a man sprints toward the area dark of the "anti-feats" as if a hurricane wind will lead to their own "self-loathing" and to the contempt of all the rest of the people.

It is the case of a man that I knew who had accomplished one of the most important feats of our society and of our time: "economic success". Was a nice, big man, sure of himself, nice for talk.

Our friend spent his months located in this area of the "Self Esteem Map" and we can be sure that his Ego really enjoyed it.

And we also know that his environment had him a great recognition, it was seen as a great merit to share things with him, and his friendship

was something that was "flaunted", many they
strutted to have their friendship.

He was a "man of action", a "practical man".
Every time I invited you to his mansion to eat a
roast, or ride a horse, you seeing the expensive
furniture of his baroque style living room and its
impressive gold, you remembered -all the time- you
were in front of a very successful person.

And when he was at the table and was talking
about other people or his past, his favorite
phrase was " no one's given me anything for free."

One day ... the dice fell badly, very badly
and their destiny changed.

His businesses started failing and he had to
sell off his big expensive house. He had to move
into a smaller house and start budgeting
everywhere be it cars, clothes, restaurants, wines
or perfumes. Later he again had to move out and
shift to a humbler locality in the town... and the
downfall continued and continued. He had to forget
some of the exclusive clubs as he could no longer
afford the membership. He stopped going for
vacations to a place that he and his family was
used to visiting for years.

The man felt very bad. But although he was
in total ruin, when he had to travel abroad for
some business meeting he checked into a five star
hotel. He did so because all his life he had
stayed in these hotels and was obliged to continue
doing the same so that no one noticed that he had
lost his fortune or in other words had suffered an
anti-feat.

The anti-feats attract despise. And the same people who had earlier admired, respected and invited him, now at the time of his downfall had ignored him. The impotence that he felt was terrible.

But what I want to show you with this example is that times the change of position in the self esteem map it's something that escapes you from your hands. You see this man was proud of his "Successes and riches", but one day he lost those things and lost his Self-esteem and their social prestige just as quickly

-29-

Outside there is a storm that whistles in the buildings and hits like a machine gun and rips branches off trees.

I finished eating some delicious meat "empanadas" that I ordered from domicile in a restaurant near the area.

Today I had a very empty day, all I did was show an apartment they gave me to sell and then I didn't plus nothing throughout the day.

An old acquaintance from school called me and said that in a few weeks there is a meeting of "ex students" but I will not to go. I don't like those kinds of meetings ... they hurt me.

And I they are kind of embarrassing those men who are so enthusiastic about those meetings.

So I said to a taxi driver:

-Did you never feel that your life is a closed room that is very small and that's why you have to be hunched all over the weather?

The taxi driver said to me:

- Look at the proposals you make, eh!

Then I was about to throw my fundamental doubt:

- Why is a person condemned to suffer when he begins to despise himself?

-30-

But let's go a little further on the "Map of the Self esteem".

I imagine you already realized: we all have one more or less similar.

And this is seen because -at the different times of life- we are all trying to achieve the same things that are what they give us pride and prestige. When we were very young we wanted be the ones with the cutest toy.

And then we try to be the best in the sport that we played at school. And then later the bravest, the that they fought with anyone and were not afraid of anything, and then those who stood up to all the women, and then the who had the highest salary, then those who occupied the positions most important in a company, then those who made their own company, and then later a wide range opens because we changed a lot, those who had fulfillment, those who they had the biggest house, they had created something nice, they had succeeded in their career, they had more studies,

they had admiration, they had achieved the most
important things, then the ones that seemed
younger and fun, then the ones with the cutest
grandchildren, later those who were most valued
and wanted by their children and grandchildren -
all shown by the feat of these grandchildren and
children- after those who more funeral notices put
their friends and family on the dedications page,
(this is joke, hehehe).

What I want to show you is that at each "age
of life" there are always some feats that are like
great "commons cheeses "that give pride and
prestige to those who they bite.

-31-

But now tell me if you do not agree with
this: although at different times of life, we were
all trying to achieve the same things, there were
always some others who went to other side… the
"different" ones.

You wonder: And how does it close?

Then it was time to say something very
important so that we can continue studying
together later on the "Map of the self-esteem".

And it is this: Regarding the different
"feats" not all we stand the same: we are
different and we have honors (talents,
achievements, virtues) different and we also have
different shame (failures, defects, defeats,
mistakes).

I mean - since we use the image of a "map" -
that not all of us are equally "close" to the same
"feats" and while one is closer - suppose - to

"success economic "other suppose it is closer to"
beauty physical". And this is for the simple
reason that one can boast of the high salary he
has and the other can boast of how nice he is.

So while the "map" is the same for everyone,
we are standing in different positions within this
"map".

This means that not all of us pursue the
same "feats", or that we chase them with different
desires.

It is as if we were all looking for water
but we were located in different countries. And
those different countries had the lakes located in
different areas.

Those of us in the same country we walk for
the same course in search of the water, but those
who are in another walk for another course.

Later I will continue explaining it to you
with examples concrete, for now this is enough for
you to go introducing a little more in ... "The
Self-esteem Map"

Let us together help each other!

-32-

I have many doubts about this that I am
telling you.

Is a chronic fight against discouragement
because every two by three

It seems to me that everything is a waste of
time.

The worst is the feeling that it is a useless effort because I will not finish it.

Start long ways and abandoning them after the third step is typical of me. Is common of anyone with low self-esteem.

I pay a language course and I leave it after the third month, I sign up in a gym and a month later I quit, I sign up for a marathon and I train the first week because I get bored soon. Discouragement defeats me

I never finish what I do and it always seems bad to me.

When I try to do something I imagine that I am going to do it "perfectly" and I start off with a lot of enthusiasm but pretty soon, I realize that it is not as good and leave it half finished.

It is this very "desire for perfection" that leaves me paralyzed without doing anything because nothing is as good as I would like it to be.

-33-

The "desire for perfection" is typical of weak self-esteem.

It is one of the ways of escaping or protecting oneself from the anti-feats. The fear of anti-feats can be normal, but when intense it can be unhealthy.

And the more vulnerable one's self-esteem is, the stronger the urge to escape the "anti-feats", even the most insignificant ones.

The most common is the fear of "the anti-feat of making a mistake".

A weak Self-esteem cannot handle even the smallest of the ant-feats and consequently, one suffering from it is always on the run.

In my case... I am very much allergic to "imperfection" and this makes me leave all my work half finished. The minute I notice a small error on my part I lose interest and throw everything away.

-34-

With this project I hope to get to the end. And it doesn't seem bad to me, it seems to me… very good!

It has its "narrative" defects, but it is still very good. They tell me:

-A man wrote a psychology book because he was very depressed and with low self-esteem ... His idea was to use his own discouragement to help ...

And I say ... great! I want to be his friend! I love!

So let's continue with this great project, don't let your patient be discouraged ... Come on, we can.

-35-

I find myself talking to a person I admire and I say to myself: *"Could it be that I admire him for the same reason that he ignores me?"*

I wonder: *"Could it be that I need his approval and his respect for the same things they are nothing less than indifferent my respect and my approval?"*

Sometimes when I see that certain people exercise on me a kind of magnetism that others don't have, I tell myself: "And what are they feats? Are not these things the did these submissive feelings awaken? "

Sometimes the opposite happens. I find a person who he despairs of having my approval, that he seeks me, that he tries to talk to me or raise issues and that I am not awakened by interest.

So I say: wait ... Why do I prejudge? What things have to do that do not attract me so much? What are your anti-feats? And that helps me to leave that stupid arrogance and open up, to understand me a little better.

-36-

I recommend that you try this same exercise.

If one day you see that you want to earn respect or appreciation form some particular person... take a break, stop & ask yourself this one question

If one day you see that you want to earn respect or appreciation form some particular person... take a break, stop and ask yourself this one question:

If one day you see that you want to earn respect or appreciation form some particular person take a break, stop and ask yourself this one question: *Could it be that I need his approval and respect… for the same reasons that make him totally indifferent to my approval and respect?*

-37-

I have among my notes an exercise that will help you.

Imagine that you are walking through a forest one day and, when moving a stone, you realize that it shines. You scratch it with your hand and a genius appears to you.

The genius tells you: "*I am going to fulfill everything you ask of me.*"

What would you ask for?

-38-

Think about your wishes.

Are there feats by chance? Very well, if there are, there is nothing wrong. It can serve to get to know you.

What feats are there in your dreams?

-39-

I know you will agree with me on this. Just look around you: Isn't everybody showing off their own feats?

That's the way people are: they strut. They boast ... each of their own feats. Like parrots. Like those teddy bears that come with a machine inside, and that repeat aloud the same recorded phrases that say: "hello" or say "I love you".

In the same way as those dolls, each one talks about his feats and says them and repeats them over and over again. As if it were the recorded tape that was put in the factory.

This book has a theoretical part, but also seeks practical interests.

His theoretical notions can then be adapted from according to the interests of each one. However, everything that I say it is practical.

And it is essential that you start seeing your around. It takes an effort… an effort signed up for an observation job.

-40-

Is essential that you develop the ability to observe.

Observing is the fundamental piece of Art. All the artists are great observers and in theater classes you teach the importance of paying attention to details, to people who walk down the street, to those who read the newspaper in a table, to those around you, to the one in the side seat in the bus.

In the same way, so that you can incorporate the basic notions of the Self-Esteem Map it is essential that experience what we are seeing in the reality around you … and leave your apartment

to life and look carefully at the people who are
in different places.

What do they boast about? Are you able to
develop the ability to observe it? What are the
feats of people who are around you?

What things they are trying to to show? What
things do they talk about when they want to show
off?

-42-

Yesterday I went to have tea at one of the
houses I have in rent, and the owner kept telling
me about all the trips who made the world and the
magnificent beaches he met and of all the
pleasures that he could give himself.

Another day I hear two teenagers talk and
one tells him to the other of how beautiful the
woman who supposedly agreed to go out is with the.
And then he talks about all the women he seduces,
he talks

how he seduces them, talks about all the
many girlfriends he had … and if you believe him,
if you believe that the feats he tells are true
then you come to the conclusion that he is a great
seducer.

Another day I listen in a bus to another who
is talking of the cups he won in tennis
tournaments and how he managed to put his last
goals. So another day in a elevator I listen to a
boy who tells a roommate college of the blows he
put on his enemy, and how It hurt and how well he
fought in that street fight.

Another day I listen talking to another of
his excellent notes in the faculty and its
"master" and all the awards it has and from his
job…

Everyone talks endlessly about their own
feats!

I think the best way to get someone to enjoy
of the conversation with me is to tell him
directly: "You tell me your feats. "

-43-

Oh, and I had forgotten those who talk
endlessly about "feats of my children"!

They don't realize but that conversation to
their interlocutors does not give them the same
pleasure as them.

And, of course, there are also the "economic
feats": those who talk about the size of the
house, or the salary, or the fields that their
grandparents had.

And I was forgetting the most common of all:
that they tell you about their "verbal feats".

Don't you know them? They are the most
common of all!

I mean those who quote his phrase.

They tell you for example what they replied
to a guy who tested his wit or your personality.

Verbal feats are among the most common.
Everywhere there are people quoting themselves
with the ingenious phrases that they threw in
different situations.

-44-

What feats do you brag about?

What things of yours do you like to be know?
What do you like to talk about when you talk about
yourself?

What things do people have to hear you say
over and over time about your own life?

-45-

A topic that interests me a lot is the
seductive conversation.

There are individuals who offer you a talk
that bores you. Yes, you follow the note, but it
is courtesy.

Many of these are those who do not stop
telling you their own feats (without a doubt the
most boring talk of all). Immediately you find
something urgent to do to be able get them off me.

But there are also those who have the gift
of giving you that talk that "catches you". They
know how to touch the vital springs of your
personality and that helps you feel "comfortable"
and that's why you let go and talk long and hard
and you feel good. Other times it is they who
speak to you but they manage to tell you something
that "arouses your interest".

And, on the other hand, we must not forget
that the same "themes of conversation"that attract
you to others bore them. What not means there are
no men who can change the subject when the
interlocutor changes and catch each other in the

same networks of their engaging talk that adapts
to the palate of the shift partner.

The question is: "How can a person build a
conversation that conquers me, a conversation that
makes me want it to continue all night?"

-46-

We can divide three classes of
conversationalists.

The Vain: They are the ones who talk all the
time about ... their feats.

The Envious: They are the ones who love to
talk about ... your anti-feats. They ask questions
about your mistakes, they always find what is
wrong with your life and they want to know more.
If you are well they do not appear for fear of
feeling that their life is a disaster to see you
well. But if you are wrong, they call you right
away, and they approach you to "investigate" what
error you have, what failure you have.

The Empaths: With them, yes, you enjoy the
conversation. They are interested in your things,
and they have a humility that makes you feel more
comfortable.

-47-

Although it is only a topic to consider in
the "art of interesting conversation" it is also
true that the Self-Esteem Map is involved.

Each one likes to talk about the feats that
are most within their reach and of people who
obtained them or also of the anti-feats that make
them more ashamed. For example, people who

they boast about "their beauty" they love to talk about image topics such as clothes, cute people, cosmetic surgeries, diets, gyms, etc. Those who brag about how well they make a game talk all the time about that same game, they talk about how well they play it, about celebrities who succeeded with it, how well they do it, etc. Those who make a lot of money talk non-stop about money, talk about business, talk about how money can be made, talk about people who made a lot of money. Those who climbed very high in a company love any conversation about how a person can climb ladders in those places.

And finally there are those who do not have any "special merit" or "great shame" and who have a calmer life ... they like to talk about general topics, historical figures, soccer players, politics, economics, of history, of philosophy, of the celebrities of entertainment ... abstract and distant themes that do not even touch our "here and now". (I like to talk about "general issues", history or entertainment ...) ... Depending on the place a person occupies on the "Self-Esteem Map", they will be close or far from certain feats. And your favorite topic of conversation will depend a lot on that.

-48-

I guess your surprise by my presumptuous tone ... but it is not the intention to be conceited. We are hardly talking. And for a while we can change the world ... for a while we discover gunpowder. We are on top of a flying carpet and we look at people from above… we think we can understand everything, but let's play a

little bit of that… like some boys playing with
plastic cars.

Let this dream take us. We have a lot to
talk about your feelings, our time, your way of
seducing, your personality, your partners, your
self-esteem, many things.

What happens is that, before going deeper,
it is important that we get used to thinking about
"feats" and "anti-feats", that we get used to this
language.

-49-

How are your things at this stage of my
treatment?

We are going to help each other!

You had the opportunity to look around you
at the world and see it in terms of "feats" and
"pride" and "social status", these three things
spread over different graduations.

I want to know if you did the exercise of
controlling your own feelings of submission - if
you have them - when you find yourself in front of
one of those people you "admire".

I mean, if you could afford to philosophize
with me and look at things from the outside, as if
we were traveling the world in a particular
bubble, the two of us, and we spoke in a language
different from everyone else's. As if we were
invisible and they couldn't look at us and we
could.

-50-

I am very intrigued to know if we really enjoyed the holidays. It seems that yes when we want them, but, then, at the moment, it is not so sure.

If one day you are lying on a tarp on a beautiful beach taking an exquisite drink while the sun is on your face, remember what I am saying.

Now that you imagine it, that possibility will seem fabulous. But if you ever experience it, remember what I ask you; when you close your eyes, when you rest lying on the sand, when the moment of maximum pleasure arrives ... What do you imagine? What things are slowly starting to invade your head? By chance feats? By chance feats? Great plans that you are going to finalize earning your self-respect forever?

In the end ... Do you really enjoy the holidays, or do you spend all your time dreaming up complicated dreams to achieve great projects.

-51-

There are people who are "workaholics", you recognize them because they never reserve a little time for leisure. They don't like to go on vacation and have no holidays or Sundays. Work is often one of the fundamental feats in a person's life. Many make work and its fruits the main column from which their self-esteem is sustained. Many organize their lives around their work. So the workaholic who also works on vacation is not really a workaholic but rather an Ego addict, addicted to success at work, addicted to perfection.

Those who are workaholics always have a job
that gives them "personal fulfillment."

-52-

I got used to detecting my "feat dreams"
with complicity. Every time I'm fantasizing about
a fabulous feat I lovingly say to myself "stop
wasting your time with that feat" and have fun
with myself. Now that I tell you ... Didn't you
think it was good? It must be a good way to fight
against the fever of the Ego that returns us crazy
... You say "stop dreaming about that feat" and
you laugh to yourself.

How about?

The idea is to stop hunching around a bit
with feats and anti-feats and learn to enjoy life
a little more (even if it's on vacation)

-53-

Did you go from being addicted to a person's
praise in the same way that a cocaine addict needs
the drug?

If that person loves you, then you recover
respect and fulfillment for yourself. If that
person despises you, then you dive deeper and
deeper into the well. You see her differently from
the others, you need to be close… you interpret
any gesture of her, you interpret it in a thousand
different ways to express a meaning and that
meaning is to know if she loves you. At a party
you always manage to pass by her side, you always
touch her carelessly, you want to know what she is
talking about, you want to know if she realized

that you are there, you always walk near her
figure, listening to her voice.

     You devise strategies to conquer her ... you
make sentences, you make different ways of
dressing better, and everything happens around
her. Even if you do not confess it, she becomes
the rod of approval for all your behaviors ... if
she likes them then your behaviors are right and
they are feats ... and if she does not like them
then they are mistakes ... they are anti-feats ...
and that leads you to despise yourself more and
more and more.

     Let's imagine it. What is special about her
that if they mention her name your legs tremble,
your voice becomes doubtful, fear invades you?
What are those magic trails that surround her made
of, that make her different from all?

     What an ugly situation! I can call it
"emotional addiction" that is made or built from
the raw material of admiration ... And admiration
is one of the most interesting and strongest
powers of our soul. Admiration has the property of
immersing ourselves in a soft madness that allows
us not to see someone "as he really is" but "much
better".

     I know you were ever in that place. And that
you filled yourself with a secret hatred for her
for her strength, for the place she began to
occupy in your life, for the blows she can give to
your inner feelings, to your own self-confidence.
You wanted to use it, you wanted to manipulate it,
you wanted to manage it to accept you, to look for
you ... and all you got was a greater rejection

and occasional expressions of interest ... and
those signs of interest were the ones that got you
up or kept you hypnotized .

-54-

How do these things happen? How is it that
our self-esteem falls down these precipices? How
did that person make their own feelings become our
favorite feat?

What if we find ourselves talking on the
phone about it? Did we discover ourselves trying
to tell colleagues that she looked at us askance…
that she smiled at us… that she agreed to go out
for coffee with us?

We bore them with details of all these
insignificant feats! But for us... it is something
of greatest importance!

We become collectors of these feats. And we
beg. Without realizing it, our attitude is
pleading and says "please give me a sign of
attention that I need that to value myself a
little more."

-55-

Later we will see more ... when we are more
prepared. We first have to keep learning the
basics.

The "Self-Esteem Map" is such a powerful
tool that it can be used for many things and each
one has his own practical interests… in the case
of your patient, his interests are the subject of
seduction, charisma, social relations,
personality, and, above all, the soft madness of
falling in love ...

How can we do to unleash that soft madness on another person?

-56-

It happens in the absence, with the imagination….

In our absence, she will remember some of our things, some moments that we live or share. She will remember our gaze, our way of being, our personality, some place where we were together, when we walked on a block or were in some bar ...

And, then, the inexplicable winds of admiration began to blow and the mind will take some of our parts from reality. And with admiration those parts will take on an unusual shine. It will draw other contours of ours that are not real ... And, at that moment, it will surprise us. We will give she a mixture of pity and idolatry.

What did we do to unleash those gentle breezes that turned into winds and then into tornadoes?

We will see later ... First we need to have more knowledge of this powerful tool: the Self-Esteem Map and more knowledge about ourselves

-57-

Many times it happens to us that we do everything we can to make things go wrong.

Does it seem strange to you?

I wrote a lot of notes on this. It is what we can call *"feat of trying to lose"* or *"defensive feat"*.

Pay attention to me.

We do not try to come out first, we do not strive to succeed, we do not strive to win ... so that - when defeat strikes us - we have the opportunity to believe that this defeat was indifferent to us.

It is not that *"I want to lose"* but that *"I try to lose"* and I do it precisely for *"fear of losing"*. It is not that *"I want things to go wrong"* but that I am too afraid of that. I know it seems pretty strange to you, but it's much more common than you think

-58-

Suppose a race, several participants are listed. Whoever wins will win a very valuable prize.

Among these participants, there is Martín who does not seem very fast to run. The face is white and the muscles in his legs are flabby. There are fifteen runners. All prepared with the adrenaline of the competition and an audience hungry for caramelises, and thirsty for sodas, who are watching them.

Suddenly, the great alarm of the start sounds and the race begins. They all run at full speed - to the maximum of their forces - while the people from the stands cheer the different names of the participants.

However, there is a surprise. One of them does not run. It is Martín who walks with a grumpy and slow pace. People do not understand. Everyone is running and he walks several meters behind them.

While walking he says: "I am walking because for me it is not important to win and because if I finish last it doesn't matter to me".

Does anyone believe you?

Actually, Martin is very afraid to come out last. And, precisely because of that fear, he is protecting his Self-Esteem with this "feat of trying to lose". Since Martín is not running but is walking, he now has a reason to convince everyone of this: for him, winning is not important, for him leaving last is not something that worries him.

Not only is he going to be able to convince the public, but he is also going to be able to convince himself. To those who say "You lost and you are the slowest of all", he will be able to answer: "I did not care because if it had been so, I would have tried to win, but as you can see I walked while everyone ran"

The other runners invest their efforts in the goal of "winning", but Martin invests them in the goal of gathering elements to be able to convince himself that "winning" is not important to him.

-59-

It is a "shield feat" that we use when our Ego is too afraid to suffer the pain of defeat. A defense mechanism against the threat of the "anti-feat of losing".

But it does us a lot of harm because it leads us to fail in the things that matter most to us. The more important it seems to us to win, the more we fall into this dark spiral and the more effort we make to lose.

And then we say *"I didn't mind winning."* And, in order to deceive ourselves, we give ourselves, like a candy for pride, all the efforts we made to lose, to come out last.

It looks like the fable of the fox and the grapes. The fox first tried to get the grapes and jumped to eat them. And he could not reach them because they were very high. Then the fox said *"Just as the grapes were green, they were ugly"* and left there with pride.

But the best example is the race. We walk with a sulky step and next to us we see that everyone is running at full speed to "win", and we with our hands in our pockets say: "That doesn't interest me".

It is very common and happens due to lack of security. Because we do it in those races where we think we are going to lose anyway.

When, instead, we believe that we can win, there we do run with all our might. There we do try our best to get to the finish line first.

-60-

The "feat of trying to lose", then, occurs in those situations in which we do not have

confidence in our forces, and we believe that we
are going to lose anyway.

And it is common in Fragile Self-Esteem…
that they are too afraid of the anti-feat of
losing. It is one of the many forms that fear of
anti-feats takes, a fear that we all feel but that
is too strong in Fragile Self-Esteem.

-61-

Do you think that your self-esteem falls
into the group of fragile self-esteem? Do you see
life as a minefield full of anti-feats that you
escape from all the time? Would you describe
yourself as a person with Strong Self-Esteem? Are
you able to face the risk of an anti-feat? Are you
capable of taking emotional dangers?

Are you capable of facing defeat? Are you
able to bear a mistake of yours?

Has it ever happened to you that you strive
to lose ... for fear of losing?

-62-

I have to confess it to you: Many times my
way of acting is a slave to this logic.

I walk while everyone runs for fear of
leaving last and I am last for that.

Especially in the "*most common races in
life*" -where almost everyone is running with all
their might-, I am tempted to walk or look for
shortcuts as long as it is not proven that I am
the slowest of all .

The fear of failure, many times does not let me search with all my might for success. The fear of failure leads me many times ... to seek failure.

-63-

And in your case?

How much of this "try to lose" bumper for fear of losing is in your life? Has it ever happened to you that you said to yourself "I am different from everyone" for fear of having to tell you "I am inferior to everyone"?

-64-

Fear of failure makes us believers in the religion of failure.

We do everything to fail so that people don't feel sorry for us when we finally fail. We are late, we do not make an effort, we do not put attitude, we do not fight, we dress badly, we are sullen ... and everything to be able to have a good excuse to fail.

What I want to show is that be careful: this mechanism can occur in more stealthy and unnoticed ways in your life, in more important things.

-65-

Thus, on the Self Esteem Map, we have to consider shield feats.

The main two are the feat of trying to lose - one of the worst that has secret mechanisms - but there is also another very nefarious one.

The pessimistic feat of Awareness.

I present it to you.

In all religions, civilizations, times, the "Awareness" of the future, or of an inaccessible present, has always been a feat of weight.

So suppose this. An anti-feat of colossal proportions is coming towards me. An anti-feat that my Self-Esteem cannot resist.

What can I do to protect myself? Before the bad happens to me, "I Aware" that it will happen.

So when it finally happens, I can at least have the consolation of saying, "I figured it out!" "I anticipated it!"

It is like a credit bank to compensate: if there is a risk that we will suffer the worst (anti-feat), then we "realize" in advance (shield feats) and this strategy aims to protect our reputation.

The student who cannot tolerate the possibility of being postponed in an exam, then "realizes" that they are going to postpone it. The man who is too afraid to have a disease, then "realizes" that he has it and goes to many doctors. Who would not bear someone to betray him, then "realizes" that the betrayal has already occurred.

And, thus, life is filled with worries about possibilities that, finally, do not occur, but that produce a lot of pain.

-66-

Are you afraid of being optimistic? Are you afraid of having projects, plans, goals? Are you

afraid to fight to achieve your goals and to get
ahead in life?

Is your self-esteem too afraid of failure?
Have you ever been able to recognize failure? Can
your fear of failure be so strong that it can lead
you to seek failure?

Have you had catastrophic certainties about
horrible futures, just because you were afraid
they would happen?

-67-

Intrigued why some of us, in the ages of
life, try to achieve the "fundamental feats" of
those ages, and others, however, many times went
after "rare feats" as for example we stumbled upon
the various shield feats , such as "the feat of
trying to lose" among other strange things.

The explanation is in the powerful "Self-
Esteem Map".

The Self-Esteem Map places us in different
positions against feats and produces that we all
have a special way of living our identity.

-68-

I promise that, between the two of us, we
will get to know each other using the Self-Esteem
Map. We are going to realize the special way that
each one of us has to live his Vanity. We are
going to understand each other in many facets of
ours that until now went unnoticed.

We are going to look -as one who observes
the planets from a telescope on the roof of his
building- the impact that our special way of

living Vanity has on our life, on our history, on our destiny, on our relationship with the people who surrounds.

-69-

The "different" at some point in their lives felt the pain of looking too incompetent to accomplish common feats and that pain moved them to look for other, rarer feats.

When losing the great avenue of "common feats", the "rare" is difficult to return to that path and the most common thing is that he spends the rest of his life seeking glory in other things and practicing a religious contempt for "common feats "

Although each age of life opens up a special repertoire of "common feats", when, at some point, "the different one" departed from the great race for being "the best" in them, it is difficult to retake it again in the next age.

Anyway: let's leave it there, let's leave that disease of Self-esteem called "different chronic" aside.

And let's continue talking that I have a lot to tell you about your things.

-70-

There is something that happens a lot. It happens especially among young people.

It is using a feat or anti-feat to label people and to build an identity.

Let us use the image of a supermarket.

We are a commodity- in terms of social prestige-, within a large supermarket of superficiality. It is a supermarket where superficial people come in their cars to take away those who they might like to have as their friends or partner and we seem to be sitting on shelves with a label around our neck.

With anti-feats people get labeled in one category or another and on that depends their being accepted or rejected by any group.

Moving further with this example (supermarket), our respective labels(say "fat") also mention in fine print what are our major anti-feats ("weighs more than what is fashionable"), or major feats... depending upon whether the label is positive or negative.

And so we are on a shelf in a large supermarket of social prestige. Superficial people pass by us with their cart and based on what our label says about us, accept or reject us quickly. They accept or reject us without bothering to really get to know us.

On seeing our label, they include us within their basket, which is the same as saying within their plan of life, within their comfort zone. Or, conversely, they discriminate against us and ignores us to move forward quickly.

There are many labels popular amongst the youth such as "the cool", "the surfers" or "the freaks". And, to deserve one of these labels, it is always necessary that those who aspire to have it perform some feats, or stop committing some anti-feats. If a person wants to be accepted by

the group, they must have the feat that
distinguishes the group first.

In some groups of teenagers, the necessary
feat required to earn the label is listening to a
certain band of music. So the youth wanting to be
accepted must listen to this band, should express
their liking through acts such as buying the t-
shirt with the image of the band, getting some
tattoos, religiously going to the concerts etc.
Through these acts the youth manage to earn the
approval of the other members of that particular
group of teenagers. Thanks to these feats, the
group respects and accept them.

We see that these rules of acceptance in a
group is what we call in this book feats that help
pass the test: these behaviors will bring pride to
the adolescent and give them social prestige.

They are feats for teenagers who need to
feel more proud of themselves and also, to be
accepted by their peers. By listening to that
music, consuming these drugs, going to certain
concerts they can be considered rebellious, or
tough and thanks to all that, they can feel proud
of themselves.

They go on forming these type of subcultures
and it seems that their members are scared. The
fear is of not to being included, not being
accepted. The youngsters discriminate on the basis
of how to dress, but a more serious discrimination
takes place on the basis of the number of zeros in
the bank account: with age, the important feats
also change.

As life moves on, adults also put labels on
people, but replace them by another repertoire of

label. And so we find ourselves with other feats or anti-feats that people might include in their "shopping cart" or pass by and continue to ignore.

All that I talk about is on very general terms... I refer to very superficial relationships. There are others much more profound who can look beyond this external show at the time of getting to know a person.

Later we will have a look at them when we discuss the issue of sustained self-esteem... but it needs to be clarified that everyone is not the same and that we're only referring to the shallow once.

This discussion on social labels was to demonstrate the social importance of feats and anti-feats.

However, there is something much more important than what is on the outside and, that without doubt, is that what is inside. From the social and external point of view, the maximum that can happen is that you are rejected or disliked because of owning a certain anti-feat or label... but from the insider's point of view, it may even lead one to look down upon themselves.

It is one thing being discriminated by others for being ugly or harassed for some other anti-feat, but certainly it is much worse that "you" dislike yourself, taunt yourself and harass yourself.

This happens when a person defines himself on the basis of his main feat or his principal anti-feat. Like a girl who says "I'm fat", as if

that one feature was the most important factor and
what defines her as a person.

People who live pinned by their labels,
proud of it, seem like cartoon characters rather
than real people. But those are worse who carry a
negative label... or a self imposed negative
label... who define themselves by the name of
their main anti-feat. Like someone who says "I'm a
failure" ... that is worse.

We are neither our feats, nor our anti-
feats. All these are circumstances that produce
repercussions, but nothing more than
circumstances. We are made of our own desire and
struggle of making ourselves better people.

Learning to observe all these things I think
helps us appreciate ourselves better, forgive
ourselves more easily, have more sympathy for
ourselves, get to know ourselves better... and to
be more self assured.

-71-

What are the labels that you fear the most?

What things do you believe people
discriminate you about? What are the things about
you that people accept?

What anti-feats compose your negative
labels? What feats make a part of your positive
labels?

Come on! Let us together help each other!

-72-

Last night I went to a party organized by my elder sister.

She is well known and respected in a closed neighborhood where she lives with her husband and regularly throws multitudinous parties.

There is a strong urge that pushes me to fulfil a sort of expectation my family has from me. For many years I was known as the "womanizer" in the family.

Since childhood my mother, my cousins and my sisters have been making an endless propaganda about my supposed success with women and because of that, a sort of myth was formed within the family circle: that I was the "bad boy".

All of it is a lie or an exaggeration, because we know that when people admire you they do not see you "as you are", but as someone "better". And your parents always tend to admire you... which means that, they at times exaggerate your few feats into a grand legend and, in the case of your patient, since childhood he was rumoured to be a womanizer and all those things.

Now -I am embarrassed to admit it but the idea is that we be honest here- all these accolades, all this myth, everything have triggered within me an irresistible urge to ensure that I make my grand entrance at these parties accompanied by a beautiful woman every single time. So much so that I would decline the invite if I did not have someone to take along. There is a kind of obligation.

The only reason why I am admitting having such basic and awkward feelings is that this can

be useful in letting us know ourselves. I think
all men are like this at some point, although most
do not want to admit it or do not notice it...
I'll tell you about some of my personal
experiences with women but... let's go one step at
a time!

My elder sister takes care of the "accounts"
department of a very good company and has many
employees working under her. She was always very
dedicated and life gave her a strong character and
an inner strength that certainly helped her in
getting where she is today. Moreover she is also a
very good person.

So was my younger sister. She landed up with
a husband earlier than anyone else & the two were
very nice to me... Anyways, coming back to the
party the best thing that I saw there was a bottle
of Château Canon-La Gaffelière St.-Emilion...
almost forgotten by those present ... an
unexpected gem. I looked for a rather large in the
kitchen and helped myself to enjoy it in the
solitude of a good corner. Then I approached the
group of conversationalists.

In these situations ... I do not know what
to talk about. I'm not shy but I feel weird at
such time, despite the St.-Emilion.

-73-

When I was sitting on the couch talking to
everyone, these ideas came to visit me. And I
meditated on the people around me in terms of
"feats", "pride" and "social status".

And I said to myself: "Perhaps I prefer the approval of those with high status as a result of their very feats that make their egos bloat".

-74-

The question leads me to touch one of my favorite subjects: charm, "personal magnetism".

But does it really exist or do we just call that the sympathy that some people have that it is easier for them to put everyone in their pockets?

Is there what they call "charism" or what we attribute to "charism" is actually the fruit of other seeds?

If it exists, it plays a very minor role.

The most important thing is social prestige ... which depends directly on the person's feats. People crowd around those with the highest status and not those we call "charismatics." Rather, those we call charismatics are those who have the highest status and they achieved that status with feats and not with charisma.

Also, when a person accomplished the most important feats of their own group and feels valued, respected and prestigious, it is easier for them to be nice and cheerful with people because they feel good, strong, safe, confident.

-75-

I tell you something typical of great talks at social events. I tell you as much about those conversations that take place around a large table of acquaintances as those that take place between groups of unemployed men or at any party. Look closely at who the group gives them the most opportunities to speak. Look at this: when a person without feats and without prestige opens his mouth in a conversation, their heads do not turn to listen to him. . And the despised one is forced to shut up and leave his sentence half-finished because another is speaking and the other is all listening.

The person without feats and without prestige then gradually becomes more timid, becomes convinced that they have nothing interesting to say, they become more introverted, more inward.

-76-

Of course, this is seen more savagely in young people because after a certain age, keeping silent like this to the despised is frowned upon. Suppose a person without status tries to add a comment to the conversation and - as heads don't turn to hear it - he resigns and leaves his comment in the middle.

Suppose then that in the meantime a prestigious person continues to speak and it seems that no one noticed this humiliation. But at that moment - when nobody believed it possible - a member of the talk noticed what really happened and, as a favor, asks the group to let him speak. And then our despised friend can say what he wanted to say ... although for a short time because, hardly a prestigious person wants to say something, the heads immediately turn and force him to shut up.

On the other hand, there are "the clowns" who are those who have no feats - neither status, nor Ego - but who manage to attract attention to them with their, with their wanderings, with their rare anecdotes, their amazing phrases. They feel "fun", but since they have no feats and are not respected they only get artificial and short attention. But without continuing to go around so many times, what I wanted to tell you is that what we often call "charisma" is actually the prestige that the "charismatic assumption" earned by feats.

Also, if you have a lot of social prestige, everyone will approach you, trying to use your closeness as a way to increase your own prestige. It is what I call "magnetism for prestige." It is the tendency to show yourself with a prestigious person to be seen and thus raise your own prestige. This trend causes those who have great feats to obtain enormous prestige to become magnets for all those who want to be close to raise their own prestige.

-77-

Everywhere, in different conversations, in different bars, I tried to talk about these things and they told me that there are other elements such as "nice people" or "comfortable people" ... and they are right about something because there are other things that have their weight.

No need to argue!

I try not to argue much, it is better to shut yourself up a bit inside yourself and look at them from the outside. But ... there may be other things. Especially the force of admiration that produces soft follies and that triggers charisma and seduction ... although admiration is also related to feats.

We will see all that later, when we study these soft follies that are behind the charisma and seduction and the strong romantic love that so many times lifted me up and carried me anywhere as the wind carries an autumn leaf. For now we say that the most important thing is the prestige of someone who depends directly on their feats

-78-

Shyness can be described as fear of social anti-feats. Fear of anti-feats as superfluous as making a bad joke and that nobody laughs. Fear of anti-feats as weak as opening your mouth and saying something unintelligent or uninteresting.

Shyness usually occurs in children and adolescents. This is because, at those ages, there are no great feats of life, and "the social" occupies a superlative importance. For this reason, social anti-feats - such as making an inappropriate comment, not speaking well, not saying hello - are seen as extremely serious errors, causing immense panic.

How can this situation be improved? By accepting these inner landscapes, these nerves, and by assuming them, then they can be better managed. Exposure techniques are also helpful because they promote emotional training.

Just conceptualizing the process and describing it as we do here is enough to achieve improvement. We must learn to recognize these emotions, the way they impact us and the effect.

-79-

Without conceptualizing and knowing these emotions, they simply carry us silently and direct us throughout life.

We go around the world running behind feats and avoiding the anti-feats. And the more fragile our self-esteem, the more desperately we dance to the beat of these mysterious bugs.

Hence we are always afraid. We live with an intense fear of suffering the pain of Vanity.

This fear is a bit strange because it is not so easy for us to notice its presence or how it pushes us from one side to the other. But we saw that one of the things we do because of this fear is "try to lose" and, therefore, we know it's a fear that can play against us.

-80-

And the fear of losing is just one form of fear of Vanity.

There is also the fear of making a "wrong decision" that has a very strong impact as we will see later when we study your method of decision making and go deeper exploring your personality.

There are many forms of fear of anti-feat: the fear of making mistakes, fear of embarrassment, fear of missing out on opportunities in life, fear of not managing our advantages well, fear of not being liked by the person we love.

Fears that are by-products of our self-esteem and that often make us live life running around like scared little children.

Now, so that you internalize all this well,
I'll show you a picture of the characteristics of
fear of Vanity.

What can scare us the most is a cocktail of
emotions made from mixing these ingredients:

a) The anti-feat.

b) Contempt for oneself awakened by the
anti-feat.

c) The contempt of others motivated by the
anti-feat.

This truly "explosive cocktail" is the worst
that our self esteem or vanity can suffer from.
I'm not talking about each of the three things
taken separately, but a special combination of the
three enhanced & added together.

So as to escape this "terrifying cocktail"
we choose from three options:

a) Avoid anti-feats with all the effort in
the world as if it were worst case of leprosy.

b) We lie to ourselves so as to avoid seeing
an anti-feat when one approaches us. A good
example is provided by those who do not want to
acknowledge that they failed at something or that
they made a simple mistake.

c) We hide the anti-feat from others.

It may be the case of a woman who has had an
abortion & embarrassed by it says she fell off the
stairs, or that it was of natural causes.

That's right: we fled the anti-feat, we fear
the anti-feat. And, when the anti-feat approaches
us, we are very much capable of lying to ourselves
so as to protect our pride & lying to others to
protect our social prestige.

-82-

The feats follow an internal logic of
constant nonconformity. They are like a horizon
that always moves. When we reach feats, the
promised horizon of emotional satisfaction moves
by more feats.

Therefore, these emotions are never in
agreement, but rather dissatisfaction is constant
and the staff is very high.

According to the values of the Map of Social
Self-esteem of our culture, we have our personal
dissatisfaction.

Today everyone feels "old" beyond their age
because teens are in fashion. Among women,
everyone feels "fat" because hyper-skinny girls
are in fashion and, among people of all ages,
everyone feels failed because the idea of success
is a central concern.

You have "fatness", "old age", and
"failure", as the three main anti-feats of today
and you see how people lie all the time around
them.

The more immune a self-esteem is to anti-
feats, the stronger it is. And therefore, all
these exaggerated maneuvers that people do to hide
their own anti-feats are signs of lack of Self-
esteem.

-83-

I go out with many women but I still feel so
alone sometimes ... you don't get an idea of how
good it makes me think that you're there ... on
the other side.

I am filled with enthusiasm to think that,
one day, perhaps, you will meet at some important
event and remember this. And in the middle of the
hustle and bustle, of the smiling people, of the
small groups of conversation, of the music, of the
smiling marriages, all of a sudden you ask
yourself these questions: *"Who are the most
respected, wanted and requested here"? What are
ultimately those with the highest social
prestige?"*

And when you find them, ask yourself the
question: "What are their feats?"

-84-

Attention!

I was looking at the part that comes now ...

It is important that you give all your
effort to understanding what we are going to deal
with now, and that you have the ability to
observe. Not everything is a matter of reading,
but the important thing is to look around you and
see, in practice, the things we talk about ... It
is essential to make this effort to truly
incorporate all these concepts in all their depth.

Worth it.

I want to tell you something: by studying in
depth the differences that exist between "envy"

and "admiration" ... we can then draw a profile of infatuation and the patterns that contribute to triggering it.

Nothing more important than the soft madness of falling in love.

-85-

The envy. We study Envy.

Let's go to a real historical setting. I represent it to you so you can imagine it better but it is real.

Edison is presenting the invention of the phonograph in front of an audience of amazed scientists. It is one of the most important inventions in human history and was just invented by mr. Edison.

Among the attendees is the French physicist Jean Bouilaud. As soon as the phonograph words stop sounding, Jean Bouilaud jumps up, rebukes Edison and exclaims furiously:

"How dare you trick us with ventriloquist tricks!"

When they explain to Bouilaud that this was not a trick but a device that really spoke and that Edison had invented, then, without losing his fury, Bouilaud continues to criticize. He then says that the dignified human word can never be replaced by gross metal.

-86-

A first approach with some questions:

Would you define yourself as an envious
person? What are the things or attributes that you
most often envy?

-87-

Since I learned to recognize envy within me,
I realized that I feel envious in the most
unlikely places.

I feel envious while in a group, looking at
a man whom I imagine to be leading a life I assume
he is living based on details such as his
portfolio, his hairstyle, his outfit. I feel
envious on a sidewalk while passing by a bar,
seeing a couple who are madly in love.

I feel envious when I read in an old
magazine from the table at any dentist's waiting
area about the lives of people who dared to live
the way I never could.

I feel envy while travelling by train where
amid the parade of beggars, the sick and maimed, I
find some guys my age about whom, based on how
they speak, I fantasize whole fragments of their
lives and then envy them.

They are minor cases of envy jumping around
like frogs in the garden of my mind, getting lost
quickly among the bushes.

They last for a few seconds and, if I'm not
careful, I discover that they disappear without
leaving a trace in memory, rarely changing the
focus of my thoughts.

Earlier they used to appear as mild,
unexplained bouts of anger towards people... but
today (I'm much more aware of my feelings and have

developed greater self-honesty), I realize that
these bouts of temper are really envy suffered by
a petty mind that last a few seconds and quickly
vanish into oblivion.

-88-

Sailors from all seas of the human soul ...
on guard and we await your respectful greetings
...

Here comes a patient and a doctor on top of
a canoe!

Misunderstood dreamers, pirates. Smarties
from the bars that teach with a glass of whiskey
about how to conquer, and about love, while they
touch the ice in a glass with a spoon. We await
your greetings as we are approaching these
latitudes.

-89-

I am very interested in the soft madness of
romantic love

What we are going to learn here can be used
for many different things, but the practical
interest of your patient is above all seduction.

And how can I not care about romantic love
if I suffered so many times, so many times I
hated, so many times I missed a woman, so many
times I went crazy and saw beauty where in reality
there was no beauty but a woman who knew how to go
crazy for her and set herself up as a the queen of
all my spirits ... for my anger, for my anger
because I do not like when I am imprisoned in this
way?

And how can I not be interested in the topic of emotional attraction... when I have so often fallen prey to the tricks played by someone when I was younger and spent all day thinking about her... it made me follow her to her neighborhood, walking through its streets with the hope of seeing her? Haven't I way too many times done all sorts of pathetic things that I hate to even mention now?

-90-

" *This, senor, is the Knight of the Rueful Countenance, if you have ever heard him named, whose valiant achievements and mighty deeds shall be written on lasting brass and imperishable marble, notwithstanding all the efforts of envy to obscure them and malice to hide them*" (Don Quijote).

From this text by Cervantes ... What catches your attention? Very good! The feats… that first.

The novelty of the language that we use is not so great ... for the common people a feat can be a knight who defeats a dragon with his armor and his spear. For us that is a feat but there are also other more current feats.

We are going off topic ... What else caught your attention from the date?

Let's read "all the efforts of envy to obscure them"… stop there!

This is important: envy obscures the facts, envy obscures the feats.

In other words: the envious try to make us value less the merits of the people they envy.

We recognize the envious because a) they get bad when someone else does well b) they try to diminish or belittle the glories of others so that they look less important.

-91-

If you learn to be curious about these things, I think you can go ahead, and you will be able to understand everything we are going to talk about in a while.

It is important that I give you a warning. The Self Esteem Map is a psychological theory that can be used for practical purposes. However, it can never be used by beginners.

Once you have practiced enough the exercise of observing your interior, knowing yourself, seeing things that you did not see before, you can use it to find your own style, which today is covered by distortions.

-92-

But now we are going to see some things of envy that, maybe, you already knew but perhaps you have never given it the importance that they have.

The first of these is this: Envy hides itself.

When I asked you the questions about whether you were envious, you may well have answered them saying:

"No ... I am not envious"

"No ... I am never envious"

Envy hides itself and masquerades as something else.

It is essential to have a high level of self-sincerity to be able to observe the small daily envies that not only hide from our eyes, but also quickly plunge into oblivion.

Usually, the envious is the last to realize that he is envious. Many times all the people around them realize their envy for their negative, ironic, or sabotaging behavior of others' successes. However, the envious person finds moral or intellectual justifications for his behavior and is the only one who does not perceive his envy.

-93-

I ask you the questions again:

Have you never felt slight fleeting fights that hide themselves so you don't see them?

Have you never honestly checked your spirits and found envy, fights that lead you to suffer for the great things of another person?

-94-

Another of the magical or enigmatic properties of envy that interests us is that it deforms the perception of reality.

Let me explain: the envious at first checks that his envied has feats of value 10 ... then he suffers ... he suffers intense pain and that pain is envy ... Then the envious, to suffer less, deceives himself and obscures the merits of his envied and then he doesn't see it as 10 but as 9,

or as 8, or as 7 .... and, the more he despises,
the less pain he feels.

When we admire ... we idealize and we do not
see the other person "as he really is" but we see
him "better". Here we are studying a force, a
feeling, a soft madness that leads a person to see
another "worse" than he really is.

Furthermore, the envious ... not content to
self-convince himself of his own arguments aimed
at taking away shine or value from the successes
of the other; He begins to speak and throws lies,
gossip or slander to detract from the successes of
the person who envies.

The point of all this is that, when we feel
envy, we immerse ourselves in a gentle madness ...
because we do not see the other person "as they
really are" but rather we see them as "worse" (we
are clouding our vision of reality) & also because
we fool ourselves by not acknowledging that we are
envious (the fog fills us our own self-knowledge).

To summarize we can say that envy is a
sentiment that has the ability to sink us into a
soft madness that is characterized by the
following symptoms:

a) We suffer due to the feats of someone.

b) To ease our pain we resort to self-
deception and we see these feats not "as they
really are," but as "worse" and therefore, we do
not see the envied "as they really are".

c) We lie so as to ignore the envy we feel
and usually seek an excuse to justify our
behavior.

"Envy" is suddenly an "anti-feat", it is a discredit, it is a shame.

You never saw someone who tells you all happy and smug: "I am a tremendous envy." On the contrary, people hide their envy and there are people so exaggerated that they say they never feel envy.

All that they usually confess to is "false envy" but this is something different. I see that you are eating an ice cream and say "*I envy your having an ice cream*"; but what I feel this is not real envy because I'm not suffering. It's just a way of saying that I would love to be in your place and nothing else.

It is true that I would much enjoy that ice cream if I could have it. But it is not true that I feel envious because I do not suffer. I do not feel invincible desire to despise you for your ice cream; which is the typical hallmark of true envy and so I can easily admit.

The real envy, however, can be rarely admitted.

What is envied? Answer: feats.

Only feats.

These same mysterious little things that are the "real bases" that a Self-esteem needs to be able to build itself. These same bugs whose adventures we have been following for a long time. And that we said that the best way to identify them in everyday life is by looking for those things that provoke the desire to "show off", to "strut".

Every time we feel "envy" we are suffering because of a feat, the target of our envy is always a feat

-97-

We envy those same things that, if we had them, would make us proud.

Every envious person is always a proud person who failed to have what would make him proud and who, to his chagrin, discovers it in someone else

-98-

Learning to recognize your own envy can help you get to know your personal *"Self Esteem Map"*.

It is that, as I said, *"Only feats are envied."* Therefore, if you envy someone, it is because they have achieved something (a feat) that would give you pride and the possibility of feeling better. So the steps of 1) assuming one's envy 2) recognizing the feat of others, can be followed by a third: What can we do in our lives to achieve what we envy?

Envy can tell us about "what we lack" according to our "Self-Esteem Map" to be more proud of who we are.

-99-

Now what interests us is to know a mental
energy that is of symmetrical effects to envy but
of opposite sign.

A mental energy that leads the person who
feels it to the following: a) feel satisfaction or
pleasure for the feats of another b) try to show
or exhibit the feats of that other c) magnify the
feats of another as a way to increase that
pleasure.

Let's look at it in a scientific spirit:
Just as sometimes we are able to cloud our way of
seeing a person to perceive him "worse" than he
"really is" in order to suffer less ... we will
not be able, at other times, to twist our vision
of a person to see it "better" than it "really is"
to feel more pleasure?

-100-

We're both sitting beside a river in a
forest, thousands of years ago in the history of
mankind ... talking ourselves with that amused
curiosity of the boys of eleven.

We rub two stones and a spark appears ...

With that, with that we intuit that if we
could develop this technology enough we would be
able to make a fire for our food ... And, as we
are curious and optimistic we dream, then we
believe that, with this technique, if developed
enough, we will also be able to make boats that
operate without sails, we will be able to create
guns more powerful than any spear, we will be able
to burn cities and operate trains, cars and
planes.

While all these thoughts rush through our
head... We are just two ignorant brutes who have
these fantasies and most important of all: the
wonder of the spark that appears every time we rub
two stones together.

It is not exceptionally difficult to verify
that the emotion of envy has the ability to
infuriate people and perhaps, there is another
symmetrical emotion there, but of an opposite
effect, that untie other follies and that perhaps
romantic love is one of these crazy emotions?

That we can we get to find out more about it
if we open the latch and keep going down that
aisle?

-101-

Let's go with the example of mothers.

It is known that what a mother is most proud
of is her son or her children. So the mothers talk
all the time about their son or their children,
about the feats of their children above all.

So much so that the idea runs that women
envy babies a lot, "other people's children." And,
it is said, they envy them with an envy so strong
that they make them the "evil eye". Everywhere
there are babies with red ribbons tied. Mothers
who are afraid of the envy of other women.

But, just as some women often feel "envy"
for their children, mothers themselves feel
"pride" for them. So the more glorious a child is
- the more feats he has - the prouder the mother
can be and tell everyone about it. In babies the
feat is that they are "cute", and mothers are

always proud of the "cute" that are their
children.

The same person who causes envy in some and
causes suffering, in others causes pride and gives
pleasure. The mother is "proud" of all her son's
successes, and the mother's friends are "envious"
of those same successes.

Stop there!

In this type of pride for the feats of the
children that leads mothers to talk all the time
about these feats and to oversize them, we have
the mental energy we were looking for: the
opposite of envy that produces soft madness but of
opposite sign .

We are going to call it "admiration".

The admirer feels satisfaction for the feats
of his admired, and to increase this pleasure, he
clouds his perception of reality and plunges into
a soft madness that consists of seeing his admired
"better" than that "it really is", which leads him
to talk all the time about the feats of his
admired. And, not only that, but this leads him to
oversize these feats.

-102-

I want us to pay close attention to these
differences between "envy" and this form of
"pride".

There are two opposite sensations - one of
pain and the other of satisfaction - compared to
the feat of a third.

Why do we sometimes suffer when we are
forced to respect someone more, and other times we
enjoy?

Do not tell me that it is not something
important: the envious tries to "shrink" and "take
shine" from the feat of his envied, but these
other people who feel pride - quite the contrary -
the usual thing is that they try to magnify the
feats of their heroes.

-103-

I do not want us to go ahead, but we are
crossing a very important threshold because they
are two opposite feelings that lead us - one for
each side - to "self-deception" and I am sure that
they are behind many things, although at first
glance it is not so clear.

-104-

Many women are also proud of their husbands
or boyfriends and that's why they tell everyone
about their feats. They strut about their
partners, strut nonstop from their men.

I'm going to show you a scene so you can see
it well

Martha is sitting at the table with her two
friends Norma and Monica. While coffee is made and
cigarettes smoked, Martha tells them of her
husband, Mr. Gerard.

- He has a salary of ten thousand Euros .
And what's special about Gerardo is that he's very
friendly. So say the people who work with him;
it's amazing how everyone likes him in there ...
he is very important to the company.

The friends throw some comments and conversation gets back general topics. But she returns to her subject.

- ... Another thing about Gerardo is that he is a person who lives for his family ... he gives us everything ... He has been the same ever since I first met him. For him his family is the most important thing in the world. He was the typical guy whom you have known since young and already you realize that he is a winner .... So, he told our daughter "*If you enter this university I will gift you a car*". Gerard wants her to go to the best university. For Gerard everything has to be "the best" and Gerard knows he can afford the most expensive college. I do not know much about cars but his company car is one of the most expensive ones... because for him everything has to be excellent and if not it's of no good ...

The other two friends every so often interrupt & change the subject, but she keeps talking about her Gerardo.

But what do the other two feel? We'll see!

When Martha gets up from the table and leave because she is in a hurry, the other two are still talking. And then Norma tells Monica:

-I was told that Gerard came to that position because he has very good contacts with trade unionists and the mafia ...

Gerard feats caused his wife to feel "pride" and "pleasure" which led her to over-estimate them and brag about them, but the same in her two friends - Norma and Martha-, caused "envy" and "pain" and that made them to diminish the same, to remove shine.

-105-

When you admire you are happy to see your idol and everyone wants to talk about its merits and you love to talk about it and you want to share your joy with all people. With the scene that I showed you we just saw it very well.

Gerard feats caused his wife to feel "pride" and "pleasure" which led her to over-estimate them and brag about them, but the same in her two friends - Norma and Martha-, caused "envy" and "pain" and that made them to diminish the same, to remove shine.

-106-

Similar things happen with admiration.

You meet those girls who choose a singer and feel it as "theirs" and chase him everywhere. Or some who admire athletes or actors: they create things about them that are not real, they invent merits for them, and they launch urban legends. And they not only invent them but also create them because they also enjoy when they believe in those myths.

-107-

In admiration there is always some special "channel" that allows the admirer to feel the glories of his idol as his own.

And in envy there is also "something else": there are some types of ties that increase the pain of others' success.

Among people in the same profession, for
example, they compete a lot. They try to take away
merit from each other. And also in family
relationships, where the family of one member of
the couple envies the merits of the family of the
other member and criticizes her a lot.

-108-

How many times a day do you feel envy?

I am sure of your answer: "none".

Very good! Then you are in the huge set of
people who don't look at themselves with enough
attention.

How many times a week do you feel envy?
When was the last time you felt envy? Who do you
envy?

I imagine your answers: "*nobody*", "*I do not
know envy*"

-109-

Now I want to present you the case of the
"admirer".

The best example I have to give you is that
of a provincial who worked his house on my topic
of cinema rentals.

As we filmed a lot of commercials there, we
already know each other well and I stay some
afternoons to have a drink and chat. Once he even
invited me to ride a boat through the Delta and we
fished a dorado, it was a very nice experience. He
is a widowed man, over fifty lengths, and (now the

important thing comes) he has an incredible
devotion to his ancestor.

Suppose that he is called "José Evaristo"
the ancestor. He had a plaster statue of "José
Evaristo" made and put it in the living room of
his house - in some advertisements for his joy we
left it for him - and I can assure you that if he
wants he can do the complete biography of José
Evaristo.

You realize that he not only "values" José
Evaristo but "admires" him because he needs to
talk about this hero all the time. In addition, he
does not see him as "he was" but he sees him
"better". As I sometimes give him a little handle,
he gives me some history classes and teaches me
how brave José Evaristo was and the important role
he played in the history of our beloved country.

He is a good man and I don't want to
describe him badly, but what I want you to see is
that he suffers from a mild mental illness very
similar to that of the "envious" but with opposite
symptoms.

Of course, he has a mild mental illness
because he cannot see clearly and sees in his
admirer a very different person than the real
person, that is, he "idealizes" him.

The admirer always has to talk about his
admirer and looks for opportunities in the
conversation to touch that subject. And, in
addition, it often imitates it.

My client is an "admirer"

Do you remember an admirer?

Don't you know of anyone who talks about a hero as if his glory belonged to him?

Don't you know of anyone who tells you about some of their ancestors, some friend, some politician, some artist, some athlete ... someone they admire?

-111-

And the charisma? Is it not also one of the forms of admiration?

I return to my eternal theme of charism!

I mean: just as the envied are underestimated in their achievements by the envious, perhaps the charismatic is overestimated in the same way by his admirers and that "overestimation" of his figure is what we call charisma ... a kind of collective admiration motivated by special events that occur in a rare situation.

-112-

Charisma is the result of a group's admiration for a person, and this person in general always has some kind of feat. The charismatic always has some "special merit", something he did or achieved that sets him apart from the rest, something that allows him to arouse mass admiration, something that makes him "stand out", something that places him as a luminous being superior to the rest of humanity.

The charismatic is always perceived as someone "valuable", let's say that he is not a despised person, just the opposite. As I was saying ... if envy twists the perception of the real towards despising the envied ... and admiration runs towards overvaluing the admired ... Is it not that sometimes admiration can be massively unleashed and make the way that a group sees a person be sick?

-113-

Another form of envy is satisfaction and happiness with the anti-deed of others.

The most common envy is to suffer for someone else's feat, but it has its counter-face: the other envy. An envy that gives satisfaction to the envious.

Enjoy the failure of others, rejoice in the defeat of the other.

It is seen in the pleasure that gossips and critics feel when they tear someone to pieces in a conversation. It is like a banquet where everyone enjoys when the failures, shame, and defeats of the criticized are pointed out. Each one contributes and those who do not criticize likewise enjoy the poison that others pour. They comfort and enjoy that gossipy conversation, with this form of envy that consists of happiness for the anti-foreign feat.

There are people who, when they speak, tend to ask you questions about your feats. They are almost always the emotional skilful. They give you an opportunity to talk about the things that make you feel proud. It may be your children, it may be your job, it may be your ideas or your sporting merits. Those things that make you feel proud.

There are other people who, in the conversation, only want to talk about "their" feats, and when you talk about yours, they get bored, stop listening, become disinterested, or, quickly, change the subject without listening to you.

And there are people, finally, who are interested in ... "your anti-feats."

The latter enjoy this form of envy that consists in satisfaction with the anti-deed of others.

They are curious and attracted to the parts of your life that are going wrong. They want to know where you failed.

They have a radar to find just what in your life is wrong. If you invite them to your house, they will look for the error, which is wrong. Then they go with that gossip, and use it to spread it throughout the city. With that radar to look for anti-feats that they have (look for your defeats, look for your flaws, look for your shame), they immediately find what is wrong, they go straight there, they ask thousands of questions, and they take that gossip to tell others people. So, speaking of your anti-feats to other people, all these envious, picky, and gossips enjoy the conversation. It is that, when talking about your failures, they say "he is worse than us", and they feel more important, or they find comfort in their frustrations.

They ask you the question you didn't want to hear. And when you answer, they ask more questions about your mistakes and failures in life. And you see, then, the indiscriminate joy that they experience and that they try to camouflage with phrases of solidarity.

Envy of satisfaction also deforms the perception of reality. Those who enjoy these pleasures and ask questions about your mistakes, do not see your mistakes "as they really are", but "much more serious", in order to increase their degree of pleasure. That is why, when they ask the questions, they look at you with suspicion if you do not speak of your failures with all the enormous dimension that they intend to give.

-114-

Para-psychologists say that "Envy" can influence telepathically as "bad energy", and push us to things that go wrong, and that go wrong in life. We will not take sides on that.

But there is one thing that is certain: we all want to be accepted. Then, with the language of gestures, the envious can press you to make mistakes and fail, to give them their acceptance.

As a result of frequenting these types of people, one can go programming to fail, to suffer defeats, in such a way as to have anecdotes that serve to speak to them, and obtain the reward of their joy, satisfaction and love.

In some social groups, or family groups, a member may be pushed into that role: misleading other group members with their failures, embarrassing anecdotes, and humiliations. It is the same that the group generates: he has to fail to make others happy.

The negative social group pressures the individual to become a collector of fun failures that can give pleasure to others and goes through life obtaining stories of failures so that they can amuse all of them and not disappoint the expectation. What's more, as they secretly enjoy the pleasure of belittling it, they will get angry and express disgust if the character tries to do something good with their life.

Something like this happened to me in my family group. He was always the terrible, drunk boy, a lost case. Then they will have become accustomed to belittling me and will want them to continue having anecdotes that show that they never went to a seminar, and then feel love, over protection and acceptance.

These groups that discharge the envy of satisfaction on an individual can "program" him so that his life goes where the group wants according to the role assigned to him. It is necessary to recognize it, to become aware and to be able to separate from these plots.

-115-

In the meantime, I recommend an exercise: sow Self-esteem.

It consists of learning to identify, in our daily life, what are the feats of the people we frequent.

You have to pay attention: topics of conversation that excite them. It can be a hobby, such as practicing a dance, it can be a very proud child, the anecdotes or personality of a child, the grandchildren, perhaps a sport, an interest, a

surname, a knowledge of history, or about sports,
an award.

Paying attention, sharpening our
sensitivity, we will be able to discover its
different, delayed, secret ... feats.

Once we recognize their feats, my proposal
is as follows: recognize them. Every day practice
the exercise of recognizing a person for a feat,
with sincere recognition. As soon as you start
doing it, you will see that the habit
automatically sticks to you, because knowing how
to identify the feats of others and recognize them
brings so much harmony, so much good vibration,
that it is incorporated into your personality and
you always do it later, without realizing it. that
was once a built-in trick.

Recognizing others is the shortest way to
practice humility and to recognize yourself.

-116-

What is promised is what is promised ... Now
we are going to talk for a while about this
Admiration that happens with Romantic Love ... and
above all about seduction.

Seduction is the Art of driving a person
crazy, because whoever is in love always idealizes
and does not see the one who loves "as he really
is" but rather sees him "better". Seduction occurs
in the absence when someone recounts a person's
memories and rebuilds them with their imagination
and from then on builds a different version of
that person. We were with her at the bus station,
we were with her in the back seat, we were with
her on the beach, we were with her at the bar, we

were with her on the sidewalk: from all that, our imagination selects the best shot of the best place.

The lover does not see his beloved as "she really is", but he sees her "much better". And I am sure it is a madness similar to envy, but with much more powerful effects.

Philosophers and magazine opinion-makers say that this is not healthy, that you have to look at the other person "as he really is" and that it is bad to idealize ... you have to open your eyes before loving. I think these people put rational explanations on a territory that belongs to the instincts. So there is no use telling us that going crazy is wrong ... once we are completely crazy

-117-

Is it wrong to idealize?

If we look at the different tribes and go back to the most distant periods in the history of man, we always find idols, heroes, gods.

Artists of all time have always created gods and heroes for their societies.

The admirers of all time always over-dimensioned the figure of their idols, and magnified their feats, or attributed feats that they did not really have.

I think we can look more closely at admiration across different civilizations and cultures. Warrior peoples often admired aggressive animals such as eagles or snakes or lions. Different cultures, different challenges of nature, and the human need to find idols to idolize.

The admirers of all time have always oversized the figure of their idols and magnified their feats or attributed feats that they did not really have. Thus some of our ancestors of the original peoples of America, could come to believe that a snake was capable of producing the rain ... and they believed it because they attributed feats, and this is due to the madness of admiration

-118-

At some point we put forward an explanation of what is "a feat" and said that it is the test that our mind has to realize that we are strong to survive in the environment and, therefore, our genes deserve to pass to the generation following.

If this were so strong ... the madness of love can be much more intense than any other madness unleashed by these winds. We do not know and it is one possible explanation among many others.

Also, one of the attributes that empowers feats is Difficulty.

Difficulty empowers all feats. Fighting a child is not a feat, fighting against someone very strong is a feat. Climbing a dune from a beach is not a feat, climbing Everest is a feat.

Just as there are people who brag about their feats, it is common for them to boast of the Adversities or Difficulties that happened.

Therefore, Difficulty is the attribute that empowers feats.

And, regarding romantic love, it can be seen that all the best known love stories are crossed by Difficulty or Adversity. In the case of Romeo and Juliet, it may be the Difficulty that both families hated each other and prevented the union.

Impossible loves are the strongest. The most important love stories of all myths are loaded with quotas of drama and tragedy that put Adversity to love. And with Adversity loves becomes stronger.

Since Romantic Love is one of the feelings linked to feats, Difficulty is a trait that empowers it, that makes it strong.

-119-

One of the secrets of the madness of love ... is that the feelings of whom we love become our primary feat or even our greatest anti-feats.

If she says "A" ... we laugh. If she says "B" ... we cry. We suffer a lot, we suffer a lot because that person suddenly acquires the ability to immerse ourselves in the deepest wells of self-contempt.

In this regard ... it is interesting that you notice the impact that the contempt of others has on your self-esteem. Ahead! It is a task for the home, because, as we said, the most important thing is to make an effort in the observation tasks since that is the only way to acquire these concepts.

You are going to realize that, in general
lines, the people who have the feats and,
therefore, have the social prestige -and that
therefore you respect- ... have a much harsher
contempt than those others who do not have the
feats.

-120-

Watching television programs, movies,
classic plays ... it is the man who "declares his
love" or expresses his feelings. And it is the
woman who, thanks to her beauty, thanks to her
charms, thanks to her skinny and cute body, thanks
to her impressive dress, thanks to her
decorations… manages to seduce the man and awaken
these feelings.

The feat of the woman then is to seduce the
man.

Keep the man in love, get him to declare his
feelings, get all these feelings towards her to
appear within him. Rather, men's feelings are
feats for women and that is why they come to need
them with questions such as "did you miss me
today?" or "you don't love me anymore, don't you?"
and others. Who did not listen to these questions
and these complaints?

The problem is ... not just any man!
Actually, for many it is an important feat to
prove that a man wants to sleep with them. They
send false signals and once they have the answers
of interest they are looking for ... they feel
satisfaction to see him at their feet and there
they don't give him any more balls.

But it said ... if we look at the movies, if we look at the television series aimed at the female audience, the entire life of the protagonists revolves around the feelings of a man. It is not just any man ... always one who has feats such as a social class, or thousands of other things ... the protagonist triumphs when she makes that coveted man feel things for her ... she feels very strong things and then there she achieves success and all the other women envy, hate, and bewildered that such a man has noticed someone as insignificant as the protagonist.

Let's look at one thing from soap operas: it always happens that the protagonist has a great anti-feat that leads other women to despise her, and this anti-feat is usually connected with the anti-feat that the series viewers have.

In the classic soap operas - whose public is mostly women who work in domestic service - the protagonist's great anti-feat consists of her social class ... being a person from a lower social class ... all the other women despise her. However, she, despite her anti-feat, achieves with her charms that a man full of feats (with power, with a well-paid job, businessman, good looking, coveted) and that all the other women want ... to fall madly in love her.

The plot is the same: the feeling of love of a man towards her seems to be the most important feat of the protagonist and she (like her viewers) does all kinds of things to awaken this feeling.

The conclusion is that, from watching movies, television series, and all those things ... we men are convinced that we have to fall

madly in love with someone and show them (flowers,
chocolates, parades) for that person to love us.

So your patient for many years made all
kinds of paper, did strange things, things that
only a crazy lover can do, and mercilessly bit the
dust from the shoulder.

So many times I talked about these things in
bars!

-121-

Romantic admiration is madness that leads
you to be seen "better" than you "really are" and
if this madness flares up you may be seen "much
better" and even "much better". And anyone from
the crowd wrapped in the ties of fantasy and the
madness of those who love acquires special
contours… unique.

It stands on top of all the rest of humanity
as if it is floating in trails of magic.

The strength of a self-esteem is important
to trigger it and does not lie in the feats. As we
will see later, the strength of a Self-esteem is
seen in the ability of a person to face anti-feats
decision and to reject feats decision.

In the case of needing someone's feelings -
something that happens to us when we are crazy -
it is an enormous weakness of Self-esteem. And
those who know about all these things worry about
not showing it, not showing themselves weak and
needy ... but the topic is much broader to
summarize it in this basic way, later we will see
it better.

Because we need to be accepted by the people we respect, when we feel romantic admiration, more than ever we want to be accepted. And we are too exposed by fear of the contempt of who we love. It is a contempt so painful that it could not be tolerated. And the recognition of our feat by whom we love is so exquisite and powerful that it is intoxicating.

You experience an addiction to accepting that loved one and leading to wanting to seek it all the time.

Furthermore, admiration has a dynamic of sacrifice. The lover wants to demonstrate "how much he loves" with sacrifices, with efforts, with demonstrations that nobody loves so much, that his love is the most intense. There is a "test of Difficulty" in trying to demonstrate the maximum love, to demonstrate that nobody loves so much, as if that feat could perhaps raise the value of the love that he feels.

As an imaginary career, the lover wants to be the "Who loves the most", of all the other possible lovers. In the face of such a godly being, he were content to be the one who sacrifices himself the most, the one he loves most of all and this was a merit that elevated him.

Of course, many times those who receive so much love live it with annoyance or with indifference, but, for those who are in love, sacrificing themselves, immolating themselves seems to be a typical form of admiring behavior - even if it is useless-.

There are people who have "emotional training". They are people who naturally, without studying these things, have learned to observe these movements of the soul. These people, although they have not rationalized it, know enough of the secrets of Admiration ... they know a lot about these topics.

There are people who have "emotional training".

They are people who, naturally and without studying these things, have learned to observe these movements of the soul.

The social and emotional ability of some people makes me think that they would have read the Self-Esteem Map with a lot of attention. It is as if they knew all these things, and knew how to treat people - be it the boss, a partner, a social bond, themselves. You hear them speak and it seems that everything they say is sensitive to these things, as if they were seeing them. It seems that they spent years studying about The Map of Self-Esteem and about the techniques to arouse admiration.

And how do they know? Where did they learn it? I think they know this, because they learned to observe the things that we point out here. They did learn to know each other in these emotions, and then they do it naturally, without realizing it.

-123-

She asks us what do you want? And we if we are sincere we would answer "*I want you to go crazy for me*"

The first conclusion we draw is that we never have to put a roof on it.

The boyfriend who gives his girlfriend security, that convinces her that he already loves her, that convinces her that he will always love her, that convinces her that he will always be there, that convinces her that he could never replace her … Gets his girlfriend to start looking at another man…. Want more! Always wants more!

She loses interest in her boy's feelings as feats (because she already has them) and goes out looking for more…. At first she goes out to test if she can conquer another ... at first she only wants to know, she wants to test if she can do it and when she sees that someone else will go to bed with her then she smiles and leaves him and keeps going ... but after so much playing this game, he ends up falling in love with another and leaves that boyfriend who had given him so much security.

It's just that we never settle when we have feats ... Not even the most important feats ... Even the men who have conquered the most beautiful women in the world settle ... they always want more ... And more and more and more ...

This is our relationship with feats because we always want more and more and more and more….

So whoever knows about the love game ... never shows a ceiling. He never says to her "You arrived" but he shows himself as a corridor that never ends ... and it doesn't matter if he's just dating or he's been married for twenty years ... he always has to be a permanent challenge ... so she always has to conquer or seduce him ... and

every time he feels something she then has a new
feat.

     You lose ... those who know how to play this
game are shown as people who can get lost. If she
plays her cards wrong ... she just loses it. If
she wants to keep him in love ... then she has to
make merits ... and if not, she may lose it.

     There it is: we have to be a constant
challenge. Not a goal that was reached (danger! If
we are that, she immediately sets another goal)
but something that is always in motion and that
forces her to display all her charms to catch us
... because if she succeeds, by chance, we We dare
to love her then she will finally deserve to have
self-esteem since she will have achieved something
really important. We have to give it insecurity,
uncertainty, illusion and fear.

     -124-

     Everyone is proud of different things ...
and that depends on our different position on the
Self-Esteem Map. For this reason, what causes some
to envy others causes nothing and admiration to
others. So as we are all different, the art of
going crazy is different as our own follies are
different.

     But to get to know us a little more and to
acquire some more useful conclusions… I think we
will have to explore a little more in our self-
knowledge, which is the essential basis for
getting to know other people. And with a good
degree of self-knowledge and the ability to
observe others, we will be in a privileged
position to continue learning the contours of this
powerful energy that is romantic admiration.

Later I will tell you a little about couples, and seduction ... and I'm sure going to tell you some personal stories. For now, I think this is enough and we should continue to talk a little more about admiration in general.

-125-

What are your seduction strategies?

Have you ever managed to make a "miss you" said by your lips be a strong feat for a person? Have you ever managed to light the flames of the madness of love?

How did that person behave? What things did he say to you?

-126-

"Mass admiration" is big business.

It is used to move fans to one side or the other, depending on business strategies.

It is a great distillation: from one tube you turn admiration and our economy from another tube returns coins. And so we have a new type of worker who earns more than anyone. And these workers are "the professionals of admiration".

They pay you to make you admire, the "great feats" are your job and the mass media do the rest. See if when you zap with the remote control in your hand going at full speed from channel to channel, you don't stop when someone full of feats appears. For example, a supermodel who has the feat of being pretty like no one else, of being "the prettiest", or a super athlete who is doing a

report on some cable channel, or a super-
businessman.

People who have feats attract more than
people who have no feats. It will seem like a
simplistic thing to you, but I defend this to
death. And notice that depending on what your main
personal feats are, you will be more attracted by
those heroes who have performed just those feats,
those who are an "improved version" of who you are
if you define yourself in terms of feats (which is
too poor Of course)

-127-

The professionals of admiration appeared in
all their splendor just a few decades ago. Their
job is: they achieve feats and with that they
awaken the admiration of the masses. The
admiration is an energy that is worth more than
oil.

I give you the typical case of the stars.
What do they do?Attract attention and arouse
admiration.

Some pretend to be "artists" but in reality
they live on the admiration of others because
their art is a feat that serves their admirers to
admire them, and then they flaunt their admiration
with t-shirts, a style of clothing and all those
things. Those writers that people read because
they have the "feat of writing well" and being
full of prizes ... they do not write to tell
something but to "write well" and they are full of
important prizes and people do not read them
because they like it but to read to someone who
writes well. They are those super-models that -
when they appear on the cover of a magazine- all

women want to buy that magazine. They perform
feats and arouse mass admiration because these
feats fill them with prestige and personal
magnetism, and millions of people admire and know
them.

If you put "outstanding feats" on any
person, immediately arouse admiration and that is
worth more than gold.

-128-

To begin outlining the general ideas we are
playing, we can then identify three different
reactions to someone else's feat:

1) Simple contemplation

You watch someone's feat and it's like
you're watching the rain fall.

It does not give you that little pinch of
pain that is envy, nor does it give you pleasure,
or anything.

You recognize the feats and respect a little
more to the one who accomplished them, but without
feeling anything.

2) Envy.

In envy there is always "a pain". Although
it is such a small pain that it passes silently
through your mind. One of the most typical
features of envy is that it "hides itself".

The tendency is to try not to realize that
you were envious. It can still be a very small
envy, a fleeting envy that lasts a second and then
disappears without leaving a trace in the memory.

3) Admiration.

Here you feel a "satisfaction".

For some reason, (some channel, some belonging, some characteristic in common ...) the "feat of others" serves to increase your own self-esteem. You experience a pleasure and, the greater that feat is, the more your own pleasure increases and therefore you are happy talking about your "idol".

-129-

And, with respect, to the anti-foreign feat, we can see the reverse of these emotions:

1) Simple Contemplation.

That is, it does not affect you. Or, it may also be other feelings outside the scheme such as compassion.

2) Envy of satisfaction.

An Envy that is not talked about much but is very common.

Here you enjoy the failure of others, because it helps you feel less pain for your own.

3) Counter-admiration

In the same relationships where there is admiration for the feat of others, there may be pain for the anti-feat. This pain can lead to mistreating or humiliating the other person. It may be the case of a mother who is ashamed that her daughter is overweight (anti-feat), and, therefore, humiliates her in public, mocks her,

and thus manages to feel separated from that
defeat.

In addition, Counter-Admiration is also seen
in the hatred that some people feel ... towards
those who are most similar to them. They see in
the other person what they do not want to see
within themselves. The mere existence of the other
person brings them shame, and, to free themselves
from that shame, to separate themselves and move
away from what they see similar to them, they
experience that hatred, that anger and that
mistreatment. Hate ... those who are most alike.
To criticize vehemently ... what is at the bottom
of themselves

-130-

Who you admire?

Who do you like to talk about? Who are your
idols?

What feats do they have?

-131-

Most people bid to achieve or perform the
great "common feats" but there are others who have
on their horizon the rarest feats such as the
"feat of trying to lose" or what are unrealizable
grandiose dreams. They are "the different ones".

They do not want to follow the path they all
follow because it has happened to them many times
that they were last.

People who have very low self-esteem get
carried away by grandiose fantasies, they have
ambitious projects, and they disregard the

concrete and achievable objectives, the rational
goals.

-132-

You realized? Well, it's true, I was talking
about "them" at a distance.

And the truth that I am part of the great
herd of the "different" who try to be "different"
for their self-esteem problems

-133-

That is why I feel close to those men who
philosophize in bars and who also tend to dream of
projects they never carry out.

I'm talking about those wise people who
believe they are the owners of the truth. And they
pontificate with the raised index finger the
indisputable truths of life even though they have
no merit to hold on to. Everyone has a great
dream, a delusional idea of greatness, a fabulous
project that they never try to put into practice,
but that takes away their anxieties and their
illusions.

Well, my project that gives me life are
these writings and I know that I will never be
able to research and study enough to support what
I am telling you, but -well- I am going to try to
make me stay "the best that can "

-134-

Have you ever been tempted by the easy way
of extravagance?

Ever wanted to run away from fierce competition with the easy way out of being a different one? Have you ever wanted to be an eccentric, a different, a special and all for fear that it will be seen that you are the same as the others but in a lower version?

-135-

The most gluttonous of this type of "candy" are the beings without Self-esteem and without prestige that crawl through the corners because they did not achieve the famous "great common feats".

Those who reached the applauded honeys -in contrast- have a prestige to take care of and do not dare to put it at risk by following the impulse of their own originality.

The same ... I don't defend them either. Many times these glorious ones become "spoiled ones of the Self-esteem". Predictable that they only try to be "better and better and better" within those same feats that they have already achieved. They are like this.

They are too comfortable with the applause they already have and they repeat the same way of life all the time. You see them as conformists and even arrogant, but they are sheltered in their own mediocrity, in the constant strutting of the "feats" valued that they were able to achieve and that place them on the path of social respect.

-136-

Perhaps it is our inner wound, our most secret pain, our disturbance, that allows us to

dive better into our being, and recognize our
individuality.

The conformism of having the docile social
prestige of having common feats, many times
silences our inner voices, and turns us into a
pure echo, a pure echo of the voices of the crowd

-137-

If you made it this far, you deserve to have
your patient tell you a little more ...

And I think now ... I can open up a little
more and tell you about a long relationship as a
couple that I had many years ago and that set me
on fire.

-138-

I remember this: I suffered a lot, uselessly
suffered a lot for "stupid fears I had".

I argued a lot, I fought many times, I had
endless discussions, I threw things through the
air, I screamed, all without any sense and to hide
my fears and make myself "the strong one".

And what were you afraid of? Many types of
fears, many different fears from each other, fears
that sometimes did not let me have a good time.

You're going to tell me that I'm trying to
put my life in a box!

But yes: I was afraid of ... anti-feats.

-139-

The person I had "chosen" had become an
uncontrollable anti-feats machine.

And I wanted to "control" it all the time so
that I don't make new anti-feats that are embedded
in the history of my life. In those days I did not
call it this way ... I did not speak of "anti-
feats" ... but now, with this language that we
have, I can realize that it was always about fear.

Fear of anti-feats.

-140-

Maybe she didn't plant them for me, but I
couldn't be sure, and the risk made me suffer a
lot.

Fear of the anti-feat that she is "passing
over me". Fear of the anti-feat that I stop liking
him. Fear of the anti-feat that she no longer has
a good time with me. Fear of the anti-feats that
he lies to me and manages to deceive me.

Many couple discussions have that source
behind: fear of anti-feats. The fear that the
other person will leave us stupid, humiliate us,
sink us.

-141-

What anti-feats scare you when you are in a
relationship?

Are you afraid that they will know you more
and despise you? Are you afraid that they will
stop loving you? Are you afraid they will stop
missing you?

-142-

Another thing that happens to us a lot when we are in a relationship that is ruined is that we are afraid to make the decision.

We are no longer happy with that person but we are terribly afraid of making the important decision to end. It is a change of life and that is why we prefer to let things take their course, we prefer to let it go with the flow.

We are afraid of "the bad decision" which, in reality, is an anti-feat.

-143-

Fear of the "anti-feat of bad decision" means that we never want to make decisions so as not to face the risk that they will be wrong.

The "bad decision" is that stream of events where one day we plunge and take us at full speed, and then throw us into a meadow of failure and self-reproach.

When we make a decision that is wrong, we cannot blame anyone. It was our decision! We are facing one of the most powerful anti-feats of all ... that unleashes a giant fear.

It is a very powerful anti-feat.

-144-

Failure after the decision is much worse for our vanity than casual failure. Not rationally - because the mind tells us that it is better to risk- but on the deep plane of emotions, which are the ones that stealthily govern our lives.

When failure comes alone, without us moving chips, we can blame luck or fate. But if it comes after our decision, then there is no choice but to assume personal defeat.

For emotions, it seems like a bad business to decide. The more fragile is self-esteem, the more we fear decisions. This equation leads us to tend to be conservative people.

-145-

Many times we let life lead us, we let others tell us what we have to do, we let counselors take over our destiny… for fear, for fear of bearing the responsibility of being the creators of our destiny.

-146-

The weaker a Self-Esteem is, the more you need to chase feats and flee from anti-feats

That's why people with Fragile Self-Esteem are unfriendly and unpleasant: all the time they are trying to excel, to stand out, to distinguish themselves. All the time they run after the glory, all the time they want to be well stopped and they spend it showing off their own feats. The weaker a Self-Esteem, the more slave of Vanity is its bearer. And less humble is the person, it is more unpleasant.

And "mistake itself" is one of the toughest anti-feats.

-147-

We live life as little children who run through the halls scared by a Monster that we believe is chasing us and that Monster is the anti-feat.

And among all the anti-feats, one of the strong and feared is the "bad decision". Who can we blame for how bad it was if we used our freedom and made a bad decision?

What we try to emphasize is that the bad decision has a very strong impact on self-esteem. So strong that to protect ourselves we use the very expensive resource of never making decisions.

It is full of people trying to blame their parents, or their children, or their partner, or the politicians, or their country ... for the state of their lives.

And that's because they don't want to assume that they are the craftsmen of their destiny. We are all the greatest creators of our lives and no one is to blame for our decisions, much less our partner.

And not deciding ... in many stages of life ... is also deciding.

-148-

There are many self-improvement books that try to help you heal the fear of the anti-feat of bad decision. They say things like "You have the right to be wrong as many times as you want."

Or else they stimulate their readers to a more courageous attitude towards life and say "*It is always better to fail than not to try*" or "*You already have the" no ", now go find the yes*"

Reading them is good because the arguments
and reflections of these writers help us to better
face the fear of the anti-feat of bad decision and
it is very important to be able to overcome this
fear to live and have projects.

It is a fear that leads us unconsciously.
Instead, when we reflect on it we see that
boldness pays better than prudence.

We have to know that we can always be wrong,
that we are always wrong, that every day we make
wrong decisions and there is nothing wrong. Every
day we manage our destiny and we are always right
and wrong.

We are all beginners in the art of living.

-149-

We have a great tendency to put the
magnifying glass on the wrong.

We judge ourselves extremely harshly and too
often highlight the things we did wrong or our
mistakes. And from paying too much attention to
anti-feats, our self-esteem weakens and the
concept of ourselves falls. We take errors into
account too much: ours and others. We have a
tendency to minimize the good and enlarge the bad.

And so we are hit by the shaking of the
implacable "self-criticism" that constantly
highlights our anti-feats and makes us passive
beings with fear of destiny. We remember our
stumbles much more than our conquests. And that
gradually sinks us into pessimism more and more.
And, furthermore, we develop a way of seeing the
future as a river of threats and not as a source

of opportunities. All this mentality is stimulating panic against anti-feats, a Fragile Self-esteem, and a submissive and conformist personality.

Fear of our own mistakes makes us conformists.

-150-

This is the most terrible effect of fear of the anti-exploit of bad decision: boldness kills us, daring destroys us.

And a person who does not occasionally make a bold decision is dead. Is dead like the stones that brush against the current of a river.

-151-

Do you find it easy to make decisions?

Could you forgive yourself for a wrong decision?

When was the last time you made a decision that could change your whole life for better or for worse?

-152-

Today I want to walk along the edge of a beach, listening to songs, looking at waves that can be surfed (I like to surf), remembering old stories, the smiles of women who have remained inside me forever enrolled and that give me strength.

Doesn't the same happen to you? Do not the old and blurred love stories that are in some

corner of the story of your life give you
strength?

And respect ... respect for the gods of
love, who so many times plunged us into soft
follies ... so many paintings, so many beaches, so
many poems, so many things that we have left to
live and so many challenges.

Inside you are all the women who went
through your life, even though they are now far
away ... although they despise you, even though
they have forgotten you, although they are in
other stories ... somewhere in time a woman who
was always by your side It will be and that
moment, that week, that year ... belongs to you
two.

The two of us, who talk until the wee hours
of the morning about love and about women ... we
conclude that it is okay to go crazy with love and
that it is even a duty of all couples to keep
burning this mysterious flame that allows both
members not to see each other as "really are".

-153-

All loves are platonic loves.

Because they are made about Admiration and
Admiration combines with fantasy and generates
myths. Whenever there is love, there is myth.

Heroes have two components: Admiration and
Art.

Artists of all civilizations were the ones
who created heroes and gods to give their peoples
the strength they needed to face their fears. The
artists drew pictures in the cave paintings to

convince those primitive men that they had
powerful gods who helped them face threats from
outside. The heroes generated them so that the
towns can admire.

To seduce is to be the artist and the hero.
It is about using in your favor the emotional
energy of Admiration from Fantasy. So the puzzle
is important, because without a puzzle it is very
difficult to imagine.

-154-

If we look at the history of humanity, we
find that the human being always had idols, he
always had gods, he always allowed himself to be
enveloped by these mythical fantasies and,
therefore, they are part of us.

Admiration is part of us.

-155-

I found that within me, although I do not
like to admit it, there is a latent need to be
accepted or recognized ... but - unfortunately - I
do not care who recognizes me and who does not,
but there are people whose applause I seek more
than others.

And, above all, that is seen when I am
caught by the soft madness of romantic admiration.

I find myself in front of a person that I
admire a lot -such as a Woman who fell in love
with me- and the sad truth is that inside me a
stream of emotions that says "accept me", "accept
me", "accept me"

-156-

The point is when I am face to face with a
person I admire a lot - and whose contempt could
hurt a lot - I get too weak.

On those occasions my Personal Self-Esteem
Map looks like a lost compass that turns
disoriented.

I don't know what to do in front of that
person that I want to be accepted… but I am still
afraid of committing an insignificant anti-feat.
An insignificant anti-feat such as a social error,
a silly joke, a little thoughtful comment ... all
of this seems very serious to me before the
searching gaze of those who I admire so much.

That happens to me when I admire a person
very much, especially if I am very much in love.

While I'm not with her I imagine things. And
what do I imagine?

Feats I imagine successes that happen in
front of her, and that lead her to be surprised
and say "How brilliant Martin is ... he is my
hero!". In all those imaginations it feels
splendid. I have come to speak alone, listening to
music, rehearsing dialogues where I have a
privileged position, full of successes. For
example, I imagine that I am going to surf the
wave of teahupoo (one of the most dangerous waves
in the world), and she, seeing me in the video, is
surprised by my bravery. I imagine that I surprise
her with feats, she is amazed, and looks at me
with admiration. All that fantasy is wonderful.

But in reality, all that is a bubble that
bursts and falls into nothing. The reality is that
when I come across her and face to face with her,

then I panic at her scorn. The fear that assails me is very powerful.

Now, more precisely, it is the fear of committing a small anti-feat in front of her gaze, and that for that anti-feat, she, with just reasons, despises me. In trying to specify it now, everything looks very silly, but at the moment insignificant questions take on serious drama. I'm talking about a superfluous anti-feat, such as being poorly dressed or that my tone of voice comes out with doubts ... that seems very serious to me and that possibility makes me panic. And in fear of committing a trivial anti-feat in front of her, I may become paralyzed.

Then that happens, I return home, I play the music, and others I return to the fantasies: I dream of grandiose scenarios where I see myself full of feats and she feels surprised.

The interesting thing if you look closely at this - as I have been doing all this time - is that, sometimes, it is the other person who is making a huge effort to achieve our acceptance. Sometimes the other is the one who makes little faces and has an enormous fear that we will despise him.

I invite you to do these observation exercises. It is important that you look around you with attention, sincerity and patience.

Learning to recognize these episodes, and these emotions, helps me a lot to improve. And it is part of what we call emotional training

The situation of the one who loves admits to being compared to boxing.

I practiced boxing during a time of my life in my neighborhood gym. And there was a man in the gym that really caught my attention: he was already very old, he was always dressed in many jumpsuits or clothes, he hit the boxing bag with slow blows, he skipped the rope very slowly and awkwardly. And he had no muscles but was flabby and fat.

So this man - let's call him "the old man" - whenever he could tried to box with the youngest and strongest and most trained. He discarded the beginners, and preferred to box with the most advanced and especially with the strongest.

He boxed with boys much taller than hers. In boxing, height is an advantage because the higher a person is, the farther his punch can go and therefore has more distance to hit against an opponent who does not reach him. Also, he boxed with boys much faster than him, and with much greater coordination and skill ... because the old man could hardly coordinate two blows in a row in his pitiful slowness. You saw this when he trained with the boxing bag, he hits the bag with very slow combinations of blows, so slow that they realized that age - and perhaps alcohol - had wreaked havoc with his motor skills. The issue is that he hit everyone ... the old man hit and everyone was afraid of him. Even the tallest and strongest, even the fastest, even the most muscular ... everyone was afraid of the slow and flabby old man. One day I asked him "How do you always hit them?" and he answered me "I let myself be hit ... since nobody wants to be hit ... I let myself hit and so I can hit much harder".

With romantic love I think it should be the same. Instead of denying how we are when we are in love, we should try to observe what happens to us in our favor, so that we can also use it to hit harder.

-158-

Now let's talk a little bit about jealousy.

Arturo is married to Laura, the "prettiest".

Every time Arturo arrives with Laura somewhere, at a barbecue, at a meeting, everyone looks at her and then they say, *"How did you manage to conquer such a beautiful woman?"*

He is proud, he shows off, he shows off. He boasts of having seduced the "prettiest". In his Self-Esteem Map, he occupies the position of "winner" thanks to the feat of his wife's beauty.

The beauty of his wife is one of the main feats of Arturo's life. Enjoy the social prestige that he receives for that feat. Enjoy imagining those comments of amazement and respect. They see him arrive and everyone comments on his wife, and he is proud. He knows they respect him for that.

But one day Laura is looking for a lover. Arturo now has the anti-feat. When they see him arrive, the same people who used to say "he's a winner" now whisper quietly. The same people who used to admire him now have compassion for him. That is, by an act of his wife, he goes from being a genius to being a fool.

Before he boasted, he boasted, he was proud ... but now he has instead a shame that attracts derogatory comments and compassion from people.

Maybe Laura never cheated on him. Maybe it's all fantasies. But Arturo suffers greatly from that possibility. He suffers so much that he cannot sleep.

But if we look at it more precisely, there are two different anti-feats. On the one hand, to suffer infidelity, and, on the other, to be deceived.

To avoid the anti-feat of infidelity, Arturo wants to control Laura. He doesn't let her go anywhere. He doesn't let her have a job. He won't let her paint her nails. He doesn't let her see her friends. He insults her when she puts on makeup.

And, for the mechanics of these emotions, the only important thing is to avoid the dreaded anti-feat. Put a strap on if necessary. Tying her up, locking her up if necessary in order to avoid being cheated on and that will tear apart her social prestige and pride. And that is what happens to Arturo who does not think about it: he only knows that if he ties her, if he does not let her out, if he takes away all her freedom, then she cannot provoke him to the anti-feat.

To avoid the anti-feat of deception, Arturo uses a very expensive procedure in terms of personal but infallible happiness: he believes absolutely nothing. An absolutely incredulous person is safe from deception. Then Arturo accuses her and insults her.

He accuses her of committing infidelity, he accuses her of lying. In this way, if there is infidelity, at least he was not deceived because he can say "Did you see? I already knew it".

It is a shield feat of "awareness". If she cheats on him, then he has the consolation of having insulted her before and he can say to himself "I ... I already knew".

Arturo to be safe from that anti-feat becomes a detective: he checks email, cell messages, asks questions about schedules.

Search ... search ... What are you looking for? "Realize", which shows that nobody takes it for a fool. The feat pessimistic shield of "realizing" that becomes a certainty that you have already been deceived.

-159-

Now looking at everything from this perspective ... Doesn't it look very simple? And that's what it's about: learning to identify anti-feats in order to better manage the emotions they generate

-160-

How many times we look for women to show off, we look for a person who serves us so that people respect us more, we look for an ornament with which to complete our image. The couple ... for social prestige.

But if our partner uses it as a feat that gives us prestige ... What if he leaves us?

What happens to that prestige lent if he abandons us?

-161-

To close the chapter of the relationship that I was telling you a little, the truth is that this woman in the end ... left me.

She told me:

-You have no projects in life, you have no aspirations.

She told me:

-We are very different.

She told me

-You look like an eighty-year-old man

-162-

It is very common that when they abandon you ... they humiliate you a little or they treat you badly ... They try to punish you by charging you with the responsibility for the decision they make.

In order not to suffer the impact of the anti-feat, a culprit is sought and humiliated.

-163-

Let's go to an example.

Jimena has been dating Ignacio for many years. She is one of those women that everything has to be perfect, 10 points. The perfect job, 10 points. The studies, 10 points. The couple, 10 points. With all the items in her life 10 points,

Jimena felt very proud of herself, and compared to friends, and felt better.

She was very proud of the couple they formed. Jimena talked a lot to her friends about her Ignacio, about how terrible Ignacio was, about the things Ignacio did, he told everyone about this man. She said she missed him every time she didn't see him and that there was a lot of "chemistry" between the two of them. She sent the part of having a partner that worked ... as well as the part of her job, her studies, her family, her income, her social class, almost all her life.

One day Jimena met Ezequiel. A very nice co-worker, and with some qualities such as height, rudeness, intelligence, authority, good humor ... that made him feel butterflies in the belly. Then he entered a period of confusion ... From then on, every day, when talking to Ignacio, he began to look at him in a different way.

-164-

It was that she was angry! Now her work was 10 points, her studies were 10 points ... but her partner was 4. She couldn't be so proud of herself.

Something was wrong with her life and she was her partner… because she was next to a man she was not sure to love. She was failing in that area of life ... unlike other friends of hers who did have a man they really wanted, who they really loved.

And it was the fault of this useless and boring Ignacio who did not make himself loved!

The very unfortunate man was so clumsy and dressed so badly and had such an opaque personality ... that he had made her not love him anymore!

-165-

Jimena was very angry.

Before, she had the "feat of loving the couple" that was one more item in her perfect life. Now she had the "anti-feat of being with a person she doesn't love," and that was the grain in her perfect life.

Now she was not so perfect. There was an item in her life that was wrong.

In life's perfect report card, she could say "work" and put a fair 10, "studies" and put a 10, "friends" and put a 10, "success" and put a 10, but when saying " couple "had to put on a 4. A terrible fury!

Who was to blame for this? To the imbecile and good-for-nothing of Ignacio, her boyfriend, who was so bored he couldn't keep her in love! She hated it! So she started trashing him, started treating him like a baby, started asking him to "change". One day, when they were having a coffee, she very seriously said:

-I want you to fall in love ... to conquer me ... to make me feel things. I want to feel butterflies in my belly.

Ignacio at that time had already agreed to change his clothes and bought more elegant clothes from the same brand that Jimena recommended.

Now he was changing his style a bit, his personality… he had become someone more "rude"… as Jimena had indicated that they had to be men. And from that day ... he tried to comply with this new instruction. He bought her flowers, wrote her letters ... (How is this to seduce? Is it what you see in the movies that gallants do?), Bought her gifts, surprised her with candlelight dinners ... and with every new thing he did, found on Jimena's face a cruel contempt. A contempt that was noted so that he knows that she despised him.

When Jimena left him, it made him feel stupid. And he threw a last missile on Ignacio's Self-Esteem that was already reeling.

Ignacio asked for forgiveness a thousand times, he said "I can change", and the only thing he found on the other side was boredom. And with each new rejection ... he hated himself more and the only way he had to "forgive himself" the anti-feat of abandonment ... was obtaining the feat of reviving the feelings of respect, love, admiration that she had ever given him. professed.

And it was a vicious circle: this sticky dependence instead of arousing admiration only brought him more rejection from the furious Jimena. Jimena secretly hated him behind compassionate kind treatment, despised and humiliated him.

-166-

Didn't you ever see yourself immersed in a sad situation like this?

Have you never let the hatred of the person next to you destroy your personality? Never

betrayed yourself to follow the instructions and
advice of someone who no longer loved you?

-167-

Today I am a sentimental counselor, but I
don't want to remember all the bullshit I did when
she left me.

We came from a long time of being together.

We had experienced many things. I imagined a
whole life plan with her. I imagined the name that
I was going to give my children. I imagined
meeting her at night when I returned from work,
and eating something together at the living room
table.

I imagined the two of us on the beach
holding our children by the sea. I imagined facing
our crises together. I imagined thousands of
stages of life that we were going to face in two.
I admired her, I admired her style. She had the
things that I felt were always denied me. And
admiration - unlike respect - always has a small
dose of tenderness

-168-

Also, when you are at the well everything
seems bad to you.

I felt that my work was bad. He felt that no
one could like him. I felt that was why they had
abandoned me. I felt that all the life that I had
armed myself had been destroyed like a castle of
cards. I started swimming three times a week to
distract myself and went back to boxing. I would
go to some small bars and have glasses of whiskey
and listen to music.

That did me a lot of good: going to a bar to be away from home, away from everyday objects, and enjoying a drink in a bar. But still the only obsession I had in my thoughts was to go back to her.

-169-

Have you ever set out to be the owner - or the owner - of someone's feelings, and all your imagination and your thoughts went to work for that? Never became a madman thirsty for the phrase "you are special to me"?

-170-

With the woman who was telling you that she abandoned me, I did nothing of what I now ask. It is very easy to speak in a bar, but within the situation, very strong feelings invade you.

... I fell for a few months in absolute and total lowering. If I could make her fall in love with me again, I would feel good again.

-171-

I was a drug addict. A zombie who walked through life with his head down and fixed thought with insistent ideas:

"How can I do to get her back?"

"How can I listen to the words I miss you said in his voice again?"

"What do I have to do to pass this tough test that life has put on me and that my plan to start a family with her be possible again?

-172-

On weekdays, with the torrent of work problems, I more or less endured them. But when Friday came ... an emptiness appeared, an emptiness so great that it was appalling.

I was afraid that Friday would come.

And all the time he was scheming "strategies" for me. I asked my sisters for advice and my sisters told me to "fight for her" and that made everything worse ...

I asked for forgiveness for things I never did! I behaved like a drag. I fell into disgraceful and embarrassing antics. One rainy night I sat all night in front of her door with a bouquet of flowers waiting for her to come out, to show her everything that I loved her.

But it did not serve to convince her.

I made so many pieces of paper, I lowered myself so much, I felt so sorry, my name ended up rolling in the conversations of so many snakes, I crushed my dignity in such a disgusting way ... I don't even want to remember. I threw so much dirt at myself.

And the "strategy" trap. The strategy trap leads to the destruction of Self-esteem in those hard times. It leads you to blame yourself and punish yourself for the result.

Strategy becomes the feat of having good strategy. And, since it does not work, it results in the anti-feat of error in the strategy. Then, because of the strategy trap, I would sink deeper into the well and blame myself more. Since I had

then two anti-feats: that they had abandoned me
and that I carried out bad strategies.

But before that, before the strategy trap
that was like a shabby remedy, he had already
developed a strong emotional dependency.

My Self-Esteem had developed a strong
addiction to respect for her ... to her affection
... to her admiration ... I once had that love,
that admiration of hers. But since I didn't have
it anymore, I went crazy.

-173-

I invite you to pay attention to "*the
dependence of self-esteem on someone's feelings.*"

It can be strong ... it can be medium or it
can be small.

It appears when one day we say to ourselves
"If this person respects me ... then I will
forgive all my mistakes and I will respect
myself."

Or else we say to ourselves: "If I can
seduce x ... then I deserve my applause." And when
we think in this way we have actually already been
conquered by that person who can do with us
whatever he wants.

His feelings are our feat ... his feelings
are a source of pride for us, his feelings are the
cup of a tournament we are playing.

You are very proud that you managed to
conquer a "special being"… and for that - and to
feel even more proud - you twist your perception

of the real and you see it more and more and more
superior to the rest of the mortals.

And then you ask for proofs of affection,
proofs of love, which in your eyes are your feats,
personal feats, feats that demonstrate how much
that person cares about you… you are proud of just
that. You ask him to show you that he wants to see
you all the time, that he can put aside all his
commitments to be by your side, that he shows you
that there is nothing more important in the world
than your person ... and each one of those tests
that You demand that they be feats of yours that
you enjoy ... they are all candy that you give to
your drunk Ego.

-174-

It seemed to me ... Did you notice those
women who value themselves only if they look
"skinny"?

I tell you about those women who believe
that only if they are "skinny" can they have pride
in themselves and social prestige, and since they
have (or believe they have), instead, the anti-
feat of being "fat" will despise themselves and
suffer a heap.

Well, the same thing happened to me but
instead of the weight were her feelings: if I
"managed" to have her by my side again or not.

-175-

Have you ever turned a person's feelings
into your main feat? Have you ever set out to be
the owner - or the owner - of someone's feelings

and all your imagination and your thoughts went to
work for that?

-176-

Anorexia helps me to talk a little about the
Self-Esteem Map.

When we talk about the Self Esteem Map, we
are talking about the general record that we all
have to identify feats and anti-feats.

Why does the disease of "anorexia" happen
more to women than to men? Why does it happen more
to girls than to adults?

-177-

If you have the characteristic of being
"woman" you already put yourself in a different
position in front of the Self-Esteem Map than if
you have the characteristic of being "man". And if
you have the characteristic of being "young" you
also place yourself in a different position than
if you do not.

As you change "age" you change "place on the
Self-Esteem Map" like the sun that moves in the
sky as the day progresses.

Thus, not only "sexual gender" moves the
position on the Self-Esteem Map, but also "age".
And also many other things that we will go into
later when I tell you details about your
personality.

-178-

The "image" is everything for a person who
"is a woman" and "is young" and that is why this

type of anti-feats hit harder in those corners of
the Self-Esteem Map.

For a person who "is a woman" and who "is
young" being "fat" has a great potential to
destroy their pride and social prestige. A "fat"
man is not as despised as a "fat" woman. A fat
woman is not as despised as a fat teenager
according to the M.S.S. (Map of Social Self-
Esteem) of the cultural values of our time and
society.

But pay close attention now: this does not
mean that those of us who do not have these two
characteristics do not also suffer our own
Anorexies, our own "follies", tailored to what -
according to our particular position on the Self-
Esteem Map - provides us or it takes away our
pride and social prestige.

-179-

There are millions of teenagers tortured
because they look "fat" and they are already
skinnier than a wire ... but they are no more a
crowd than adult men who suffer because they look
"losers" even though they have already achieved
great success in their lives.

To realize that it is the feat of being
"skinny" what is behind the Anorexia, we can look
at one thing: they compete to be skinnier, and
feel envy and pain when they discover another
anorexic girl who is even more skinny. They
compete! And the balance is the referee. They take
photos of their skeletal bellies and upload them,
proudly, to the internet. This envy they feel when
they see another skinnier girl shows that it is
"the feat of being skinny" that is behind this sad

disease. Being skinny as a "feat" while thinness
is social prestige and causes pride.

-181-

It would be great if men and women learn to
fight our feelings of self-compassion. It would be
very good if we detach ourselves from these
"ideals" that the media set and that make us lose
the sense of what a normal life is. We have
problems with low self-esteem and we judge
ourselves too harshly. We set ourselves irrational
goals and then punish ourselves because we feel
that we cannot achieve them.

We are too demanding of ourselves and we are
running after exceptional feats. What happens is
that the media convince us that this is "normal"
and that we are the rare ones. And the way we
judge ourselves is unfair: putting too much
emphasis on our mistakes and not paying due
attention to our merits.

We are in an Economy of Vanity where it is
a business to raise the mass admiration of the
crowds and there are some characters who are
dedicated to performing feats and having an
exceptional life ... all of that crushes us, makes
us believe that we are insignificant because the
presence that Professionals of admiration have in
our existence -invaded by the media- it is so big,
it is so strong, so noisy ... that they seem more
real to us than the ordinary people around us.

We must learn to enjoy our little victories
... or our great victories. And the most important
thing of all is to assume that we live in a very
toxic habitat for our self-esteem and that is why

we must be alert. And we should not lower our arms
against these collective diseases

I am convinced that everyone is a little
crazy, a little depressed, a little frustrated ...
and that in the way of so much madness for Vanity
we miss the opportunity to enjoy life, to enjoy
affections, to enjoy the beauty that is in many
things that we do not see because of how depressed
we are. And our comparison stick can be these
strange beings of abnormal life that appear in
magazines and on cable channels and that we know
more than our friends. Thus we are going crazy, we
are filling with anguish, and with fear, we are
becoming beings without Self-esteem who are afraid
to live life.

This Vanity society crushes us, makes us
automata, makes us give up our freedom, makes us
fear our decisions, makes us judge our mistakes
harshly, makes us minimize our successes.

-182-

Has this competitive and media world ever
turned you against the messy bed of depression?
Didn't you ever feel that for not having a feat -
call it hyper skinny or super successful - ... you
were worth nothing?

Are you not confused what is a normal life
of what is a life of feats by the reports, the
biographies, the radio channels, the Internet
pages?

-183-

Discouragement is much more common than
everyone thinks. It hides because joy

(superficial, ostentatious, false) is our
obligation, "security" is what is expected of us,
"excellence" is our prison. Depression scares
customers away, puts bosses in a bad mood, drives
away friends, drives women out of love ... sinks
us ... depression is a pit. We are not sincere. We
lied. And no one can admit that he is down, that
he is tempted to drop his arms, that he does not
feel as strong as his obligation is. We fool
ourselves with brand name clothes and expensive
technology to not realize that we are depressed.
We watch thousands of hours of television and we
play to believe that we are "similar" to any of
the professionals of admiration that the screen
shows us ... and all to forget

-184-

As our Vanity Economy found in girls with
complex of "fat" a good niche to sell all kinds of
unnecessary things, the same is also done with
this multitude of people who suffer from Anorexia
of Success and feel the complex of being " failed
"or" losers ".

The message is the following: "If you buy
such a product from me, then you are no longer a
loser." And our mass of anorexic, like a meek
flock of lambs, is behind these glitters, these
exotic expenses, these "luxuries", which allow
them to demonstrate to their friends that they
"are also successful" and above all to prove it to
themselves.

The gates of heaven of the "winners" have
keys that the Vanity Economy sells you dearly but
you pay them and everyone can see "how good you
are" and how "successful you are".

-185-

Will you not be in the clutches of a black mirage that makes you see a fantasy regarding some great shame you feel or some great defeat?

What if the way you look is bent by the twisted mirrors of madness? ...

Above all, it is very important to become aware of this: alteration of the perception of reality. We see reality with a gray veil on many occasions, and especially when it comes to anti-feats. It serves to consider it, to be alert, and to question some thoughts that stun as if they were certainties.

-186-

I'm walking down the street and I see that people don't walk, people run.

I see men running with their faces wet with sweat, they run desperate and push you past. And they run after the feats that they never achieve and thus their lives are passing. They run with tremendous envy to those who have that, which they can never achieve even though the media shows them that it is very easy, at their fingertips, so easy that only a fool could not achieve it.

And it is useless because, although some pursue "dreams" (those are still alive), the vast majority reach a point in their life when they are only "escaping."

... They no longer have dreams, they no longer have projects. They are only fleeing from the great anti-feats of our time.

-187-

We do not see reality and we live in a cloud
far from everything that is true, we live inside a
movie and we sacrifice our lives ... our happiness
... our best moments.

-188-

Shouldn't we be free, humble, happy and full
of concrete projects for us?

Come on, let's help each other!

-189-

The man of today seems trapped in a madness
where he only seeks to "look at himself" and
"admire himself", and then "admire himself a
little more", and then "admire himself a little
more" and so on to infinity.

As you will notice, part of the plagiarism
that Al Pacino makes the Devil say in that
masterful film we all saw: The Devil's Advocate.

And well, don't forget that at the end of
the movie, Al Pacino's mouth says: "Vanity ... my
favorite sin."

-190-

I liked the image that the Devil uses in
that movie to talk about the Ego: "the natural
drug".

Al Pacino gives voice and begins to describe
"the icons of the modern world" with a look that
is exact.

He talks about the tall buildings, the
infinite riches of some men, he talks about the
great advances in technology and science, about
all those fabulous things, like colored mirrors,
like weak pretexts that men have to caress the
Ego. He talks about all the monumental things in
the world as "excuses" that the men and women of
our time invented to walk here and there with
monumental Egos held on top of all these things.

In other words, the buildings themselves are
nothing more than feats.

The Ego, "the natural drug".

-191-

I loved that idea. As the cocaine addict
gets excited about that white powder, the Ego
addict, on the other hand, goes out of his way for
the feats that feed him and make him bigger and
bigger.

It is a race that never ends because you
always want more ... Even if you believe that,
when you achieve the feats, there you will be able
to rest and be happy ... at that moment another
horizon of feats arrives and your Ego continues
demanding more and more and more and more.

Let's think about those great stars that
achieved everything in life ... they are
destroyed, they no longer feel desire, they no
longer have aspirations ... And they take drugs
with all kinds of crap.

Let's think of people who achieved great
feats. Those who reached the Tops of the World.
Those of us who respect and admire so much for

their feats ... How do you feel about the fear of
losing everything?

-192-

The Ego addict cannot look in the mirror and
say "I admire myself more" and then "I admire
myself a little more" and then "I admire myself a
little more" because, in order to increase his
self-admiration, he needs feats. You need to own
those immense buildings, or amass those
unimaginable fortunes of which the lips of the
masterful actor spoke.

Many have killed themselves because of their
Ego addiction. And it is not surprising that -like
other drugs- the more you consume it, the stronger
and more vibrant the need to continue consuming.

-193-

The good thing is learning to have a good
time ... learning to enjoy yourself.

Learn to say to each other affectionately:
"Stop wasting time with that feat" every time a
grandiose plan fills us with fever, or to say to
ourselves: "Stop scaring yourself with that anti-
feat" when we suffer from the fear of a great
defeat to the that we feel close.

Pay attention to these bugs. Pay attention
to your friend who one day bought some watercolors
and began to meditate in the wind.

-194-

…Are you there?

…I got bored.

        This is the second sentence after a long
time ...

        A little over a year has passed since I
abandoned everything. I stopped believing in "our
project" and thought it was not taking me anywhere
... I stopped believing, the magic was lost.

        I was discouraged and I felt sorry for
everything I told you, discouragement defeated me.
I struggled ... but I failed once more and
stumbled and fell down the pit of strong despair.
Everything seemed crazy to me ... I was even
ashamed ... as I am very ashamed of my life ... my
existence ... my own person. Everything made me
feel ashamed and embarrassed.

        And, when the lack of self-esteem deepened,
everything I was telling you seemed silly. A
ridiculous thing and without any sense or flight.
And also, I felt a great spiritual emptiness ...
and the feeling that everything is useless and
worthless... So everything gave me a lot shame and
I got depressed ...

        I left everything as it was and tried to get
on with my things.

        -195-

        And why do we talk again?

        Because you are there.

        Because you are real to me. You are too real
and I feel that "you are there" ... on the other
side of the wall ... behind the coordinates of
time and space that separate us. And yes: I feel
that "you are very real" and that you like me to
continue with "our project".

You are very real to me and thanks to that
... now we can continue.

I hear your words "Martin ... We are going
to help each other!"

-196-

Did I propose before we pretend that you are
my doctor and that I entered your office and lay
down on your couch to talk to you?

Well ... now I propose that we both play to
come to my house to find me. As I got discouraged
and left the treatment and left everything in a
bun in my closet ... one day you missed me. And
you came knocking on the door for us to continue
what we had started.

You rang my bell and said,

-I'm here because everything you told me
helped me a lot to get to know myself ... And I
want us to continue with your treatment ...

-197-

Pass.

I live in an old PH that I bought many years
ago with the money from an inheritance. Carefully
climb the ladder. It's a little dark isn't it? But
I am not careless ... I had it painted recently to
make it look better.

Comfortable.

Does it seem a bit old and ugly to you? For
me it has its charm.

The good thing is that there are no expenses
and taxes are very low. And that is necessary for
a person with no fixed income like me. It's a bit
dark ... but I took care to fix it with my
decoration "touches". Here's the door.

-198-

Do you like furniture? Did you see the plant
that I have in the living room? How about? In the
spring it brings out some flowers that fill
everything with perfume. The "Art and Decoration"
people from the producers helped me a lot to get
good furniture at a special price ... Furniture
from highly respected designers.

I chose them carefully because I really like
decorating magazines.

You're asking the question: "What are those
stones?"

I answer you: for some years I was a
backpacker.

I ran my finger through all of southern
Argentina and some northern provinces. And, in
each province, I chose a place; next to an empty
route ... a route that kept me stranded for hours
or days and I picked up a stone that has the
strength of that moment, of that story. And there
I have them and every time I see them ... memories
appear, memories of stories, memories of empty
routes and fields full of endless grass.

When I bring my son to my house, he loves to
play with those decorations.

-199-

Backpackers say that it is very difficult
for a person who did not live those experiences to
understand what it means, or imagine what it is
like to be on the side of a route from a very
distant and lost place, alone. With a wind so
strong that it pushes you on the pavement. And
waiting for a car to pass or a truck to pass.

They do not imagine what vertigo is: maybe
no car will pass, you are alone next to a beetle
who walks on the pavement of the route. They can't
imagine what it's like to talk to truckers on
long, empty, quiet roads. When you get back,
people then look at you like it's all the noise
the rain makes as it falls, or it doesn't matter.

Well ... I do not escape the average. I am a
storyteller of feats like everyone else.

-200-

There you have your chair so that you feel
as relaxed as possible. It is the blue chair.

Do you want a glass of coca? I tell you that
I always write on the terrace where you can see
the cars go by.

You don't know how happy I am to see you
here ... you can't imagine everything you give me
... the strength you're giving me.

Thank you very much for being here. I have
few guests and they are always welcome, but no
surprise is as beautiful as the one you gave me
today. It's a little cold don't you think?

I'm so excited to have you here today! It is
that the autumn afternoon brings me very cold on
these cold walls.

Do you hear the noise of the cars?

Wait a little while I go to the kitchen ...

Do you want a tea or a coffee?

-201-

… In this little folder that I have here, I wrote some notes last year on the only topic that we needed to complete everything about the great Map of Self-Esteem.

And it is something fundamental that I want to talk to you about now: "The Humiliation".

-202-

A few months ago I suffered "The Humiliation" firsthand at my job. And still today I am struck by his hard blow.

I tell you:

One day a man I didn't know calls me and introduces himself as the location manager of a production company. He gives me his first and last name and the details of the producer. This producer is very important, but I had never worked with them before so the news seemed great to me. He tells me that they had told him about me and that they were looking for certain types of houses for a shampoo advertisement.

As always, I go to my image bank and email a list of three houses that more or less fulfilled what he was looking for. She calls me after a while and tells me that one was very interested in the director of the commercial, that if we couldn't go "tomorrow" to see her.

I call the owner of the house, ask him what time is right for him and then I call the location manager and we arrange at 5 in the afternoon to be at the door of the house. The next day I am there on time waiting for the production company to come. As time passes and they do not appear, I ring the bell for the owner of the house and he makes me stop for coffee.

A tense half hour passes and the location manager calls me on the cell phone and tells me that "he had a problem with the director" and that they were delayed. He apologizes and tells me that he will not be able to go see the house today, unless we fix it at 7 in the afternoon.

Almost an hour and a half to go. I apologized to my client and, well, my client accepted, so we were both waiting for the appointed time.

-203-

The people at the production company were snubbing me in the eyes of my client.

An awkward situation. I did not know what to talk about to make us more happy. Also, this man yawned in front of me and his eyes closed from the dream. He offered me some cookies and complained, with some reason, that it was my fault that he had missed his nap. We spent an hour where I, like a dog, tried to bring up topics of conversation to make him likeable and he, meanwhile, barely answered me with a few words and conveyed his boredom and contempt.

He was my client and I was getting lousy!

-204-

Let's see the effect of "The Humiliation".

They trashed me in front of a client, made
me look stupid, made me waste time and made me
feel how little I am worth.

It is an anti-feat: it attacks "pride" and
"social prestige"

But, unlike other anti-feats, it happened
between two people.

Humiliation then is the "social anti-feat".

In all ages of human history, there has
always been humiliation and there has always been
a type of person who loves to humiliate. However,
now the preferred channel is money, so the hard
truth is that it is convenient for you to get it
because otherwise you will always be exposed to
being humiliated by those who have it.

-205-

The two preferred areas of humiliation are:

a) work.

b) the family.

-206-

The preferred instrument of humiliation in
our day is money ... since we all need money,
sometimes we have to suffer humiliations to earn
our bread. Money runs throughout society
humiliating from head to head.

The manager is humiliated by the president and the employee is humiliated by the manager ... and then the employee arrives at his house and since he has the money and is the support of the home ... he uses it to humiliate his children and his wife and so he is discharged of how bad it feels.

When there is someone with power above you, who always humiliates you (be a family member or a boss or a client or whatever), the most common thing is that your executioner alternates his humiliations with good treatment ... and so it does not seem so serious.

Over the years this thing of receiving chronic humiliations begins to leave you with the most defeated gaze, the most doubtful tone of voice, the most hunched back, the least common smile, the most famished enthusiasm.

-207-

I would like to paint you a portrait of what the typical humilliator is - the typical self-esteem killer - but the most important thing is that he loves "power".

You need to surround yourself with symbols that display your power as luxuries and your whole life the bet to have more and more power, more power, more power.

-208-

But, although it seems strange to you, most of the time the Self-Esteem Killer is convinced that he is an excellent person.

Since he is a fan of feats, he needs to convince himself that he is good at everything. For this reason, he believes that he also has a good heart and self-justifies his evil with all kinds of internal excuses. There are some who are already going to extremes and are rapists and serial killers and have a double life ... but the vast majority of them spend their days with the respect of the people and the internal belief that they are "good".

-209-

The most important characteristic that a person's personality has is its "primordial feat"

From your personal and own Self-Esteem Map (we are going to talk about the formation of the personality) and above all from his special "position" within it, what I am calling you as a "primordial feat of life" is born.

And in self-esteem killers it's about humiliating. They love to humiliate. The primary feat of the Self Esteem Killer is ... humiliating. They need enemies, and if they don't have them then they invent them. When they meet an enemy, they humiliate and humiliate him and feel better if they have ethical excuses to justify this way of proceeding.

-210-

But to know how to face a humiliator it is very important to practice emotional training.

It consists of learning to recognize our emotions, and learning to manage them, and learning to recognize other people's emotions. It consists of opening our eyes and "seeing" all these forces that we have been seeing and studying.

Lots of people spend their entire lives obeying emotions they don't even know, because they are emotions that push them subconsciously.

Emotional training is 1) recognizing emotions 2) managing them 3) being able to develop the strength to disobey them 4) learning to recognize emotions in the other person as well.

Regarding 4) it is not as simple as it seems. It requires learning to truly "listen" to the other. It requires an interest in the other. But there are many practical benefits to be gained from progressing in this ability to see emotions and their influence.

-211-

With ties of economic dependency, those in power use humiliation to suck the blood of the Self-Esteem of those under their command. We see it in the use of language.

If an entrepreneur says, "I give a thousand people a job," we already realize that these people are being disrespected. We realize that he uses his economic power to humiliate these people and make them believe that he is more respectable and admirable. A blood suck that one Self-esteem does to the other with the use of power ... of the economic need of these people for a salary and to submit to their orders.

The correct thing would be to say: *"I created a business opportunity that allowed 1000*

*people to earn a job with their effort, with their
study and with their merits.*" Instead of saying "I
give you work" ... the correct thing is to say
"*you earned a job with your ability, your effort,
and your results.*"

-212-

We must learn to know humiliation, we must
learn to detect it (sometimes wears very subtle
clothing) in order to save our self-esteem and
that nobody steals our enthusiasm, confidence in
us, that nobody annuls our personality, let no one
take away our style. And if one day we discover
that they annulled us, that they destroyed us,
that they took away the desire to live, the desire
to create, the desire to express our special way
of being, the desire to have projects.

-213-

And what place does humiliation have in your
life?

Are you in a "place in the world" where you
are protected from "chronic humiliations"? Who
humiliates you?

Who has power over you?

-214-

It's a little cold don't you think?

Wait, I'm going to go close the window.

-215-

I have great news: are you ready? ... Now we
are going to penetrate something very important

and delicate: your personality, the formation of
your style, your way of being ...

Let's study, with the Self-Esteem Map in
hand, your personality. In the summer it seems to
me that we are going to chat on the terrace. Maybe
I have some chairs and a table there so we can
both talk quietly.

Did you see the mini library I have there?

-216-

As always ... let's start with the preferred
theme: "Admiration".

Something that says a lot about "your
personality" and your values is ... your
admiration. Knowing who are the people you admire
today and what feats they have ... I can guess a
lot from the position in which you feel located
with respect to the Self-Esteem Map.

-217-

Let's say it with all the letters: "your
idols" ... are a key factor in your personality.

-218-

Who do you admire?

What feats do they have? What things in
common are there between your place on the Self
Esteem Map and your idols? Who do you pay more
attention to?

-219-

A much more decisive weight than your
current idols was held by the people you had as

"idols" during the first times of your arrival in
the world ... Your first idols ... The first
people you admired ... Admiration is a very
powerful energy.

Your first idols ...

-220-

And who am I talking about? And yes ... from
your parents. Until at least ten or fifteen years
old, your parents were your idols, your heroes.
There was nothing you didn't do other than imitate
them or get their acceptance and applause.

-221-

It may not seem so clear now, but, at one
time in your life, your parents were "your
ultimate idols."

But ... What is the most important thing
that a person can have so that you respect them
... Do you admire them?

-222-

You guessed it! Your parents had ... feats!

They were tall and strong. They knew how to
cross the street alone. They handled televisions
and cars. They spoke fast and understood the
world. They were able to speak to other tall and
strong beings. They read and wrote. They could
lift a chair by hand. They could run fast. They
could kick a ball far away. They could lift you up
in the air.

At those ages, all that seemed impossible
and wonderful. You looked at them as tall, cool

beings, capable of facing the mysterious world. Actions that seem simple to you today like driving a car were, in your child's eyes, feats ... great feats.

-223-

You looked at them with "admiration", you saw them as your idols, your heroes. And this could not be otherwise because they exhibited to your eyes monstrous triumphs. You looked at them in amazement and they seemed very prestigious.

In front of them, you had the typical behavior of every "admirer". On the one hand, you "imitated" them because the more you looked like them, the more proud you could feel proud of that. And, on the other hand, you were looking for his "approval" and his "esteem" ... and you were a chronic need of that approval.

You said to yourself *"I'm a great because I do this just like dad"* or you said to yourself *"I'm a phenomenon because mom loves me"*.

Also, you always talked about them. Like every admirer, you loved to talk about the great things they had accomplished ... You loved to count their feats, oversize them, polish them, and exaggerate them.

-224-

But one day you found out they were normal people ... flesh and blood people.

Their feats began to lose "shine" and "magic" because they no longer caught your attention.

You did not see them so "tall" ... because now you had the height of them. You didn't see it that strong… now you could lift a chair with your hand and you could run just as fast. It was not so surprising that they speak with strange and strange words, now you could also speak just as fast as them.

You were no longer amazed that they drive a car ... you could also do it. You were not moved that they can kick a ball very far, now you could also kick just as far.

And that was a very special moment for your life. It was a time when you "realized" that they did not deserve to be "your heroes" because they were nothing but normal people like everyone else.

-225-

When their feats faded and lost brightness and magic to your eyes it was a very special and very difficult time.

You lived in a kind of great "revolution" where your favorite feats were those that served to show you that you no longer imitated them and that, in addition, you could do without their esteem. If they threatened to stop you from approving if you had a behavior, then you needed to do just that to demonstrate and demonstrate that you had left the previous stage and that then you no longer wanted their appreciation.

-226-

Then, for the first time in your history, something we can call "Political Attitude" was born.

Political Attitude is the attempt to change the Self-Esteem Map and build a new Self-Esteem Map that has more generous values with what one already is.

For example, a doctor who tells you "Doctors are the most useful thing that humanity has" is in a Political Attitude because he tries to give value to a feat that he himself has ("to be a doctor"). A woman who tells you "Women are smarter than men" ... is Political Attitude. Try to advertise so that a Self-Esteem Map is born where women are most valued ... and she is a woman.

A man who feels unsuccessful and says "the winners are all thieves" also falls into Political Attitude because he wants to take away value from what he is not. He wants a new Self-Esteem Map where achievers are less valued.

A person who came out of a terrible illness by force of will who tells you "*The most important thing a person has is his will*" also falls into Political Attitude because he wants to give value to his own trait.

-227-

Many times we choose a trait of ours and give it value.

If we are low we discover ourselves speaking in favor of the lows. If we are restless one day we say that it is very important to move. If we are poor another day we are saying that only the poor are honest.

It is what I am called the "Political Attitude".

Political Attitude is seen as an attempt to campaign to change the Self-Esteem Map and generate a new one where the own conditions and characteristics are more valuable, so that the feats themselves are more recognized and the anti-feats themselves are less despised or no longer anti-feats.

If we observe ourselves carefully, we will find that the "Political Attitude" is very common, it is something everyday.

Many people speak and develop arguments to give value to their own characteristics. One of the most common forms of Political Attitude is "self-praise advice." The typical counselor who gives you advice on how to lead your life. These are tips that praise his own life, the decisions he made in his life, are ways to throw flowers at himself.

I invite you to stop and carefully observe the Political Attitude in your daily life, in the people around you, in your ties.

It is very important, to continue evolving in the understanding of the Self-Esteem Map, to learn to identify the "Political Attitude" and the first thing is to be a good observer with ourselves.

-228-

What are your most common Political Attitudes now? What presence does Political Attitude have in your special way of living Vanity?

What traits of yours do you advertise? Your sexual gender? Your skin color? Your nationality? Your profession? The way you are? Your studies? Your nationality? Your origins? Your philosophy of life?

-229-

There are characteristics that move the position on the Self-Esteem Map and make some feats and anti-feats have a different weight. There are characteristics that attract esteem or contempt in some environments.

Everywhere, there is a Political Attitude that tries to change the Self-Esteem Map and build a new Self-Esteem Map that recognizes more women. Everywhere we hear that we live in a "macho society" ... and that is a way of saying that our values are "macho" ... that our Self-Esteem Map is "macho".

There are other Political Attitudes in defense of other values.

Now there are those fashion shows where those who are too skinny are prohibited from entering, as a way to devalue the feat of excessive thinness. These parades are supported by all the people who feel pressured and need to change the Self-Esteem Map and make one less demanding in terms of thinness.

There are millions of Political Attitudes everywhere. From the most naive of the boy who says that boys are more awake than adults, or the older man who says that times past were better ... to others more subtle and difficult to observe.

Many people feel overwhelmed because they
have a characteristic that is anti-feat according
to the Map of Social Self-esteem, sometimes they
resort to Political Attitude to change those
values. Of course they do it subconsciously, and
without realizing the emotional factors involved.
They think they are arguing with ideas of
intellectual importance, but the important thing
is the emotions. And it's about Political
Attitude: a spontaneous attempt to change the
M.S.S (Map of Social Self-Esteem) through a speech
that tries to combat hegemonic values and supplant
them with new ones.

-230-

It is very important and very practical that
you learn to identify the Political Attitude in
yourself, in your speeches, and in the people
around you.

Political Attitude can be very useful to
build magnetic speeches and to better communicate
an idea, giving it emotional value. It is also
important to do so in order not to engage in long
intellectual discussions about ideas, about
arguments that, deep down, have a much more
decisive and closed emotional background.

Over time, if you learn to identify
Political Attitude, you may even develop the
ability to recognize characteristic facial
gestures. You learn knowledge that helps you
interact, prevents you from uselessly hurting
other people's feelings (something we do
involuntarily, subconsciously) and can also help
you in your persuasive powers.

For this reason, if you have not understood it, I would recommend that you review it. And that you can learn to identify Political Attitude (attempt to change The Self-Esteem Map for a new one where our own anti-feats have less anti-feat value, and our feats have more feat value, generally through spontaneous speech)

-231-

It is important, to understand the Self-Esteem Map, to complement the theoretical incorporation of these concepts, with practical observation of our interior and the reality that surrounds us.

An excellent place is elevator travel. It is incredible but with asking a question about the time, talking about the weather... it is enough for the person in front of us to dispatch many times with a waterfall of feats. If they see you young, they tell you forty-seven feats of their life even though they do not know you and without considering that it is a simple elevator talk.

You have to pay attention to these things ... you have to observe reality to finish understanding the Map of Self-Esteem

-232-

One of the favorite feats of fathers and mothers is to be "the best father in the world" or "the best mother in the world".

They use their children as an instrument that serves to fill their lives. They have an empty life and with exaggerated gestures of over-protection they find a reason to feel pride and social prestige.

These people talk about their children all the time. They talk about everything they do for their children. They talk about everything they sacrifice for their children. They talk about all the effort they make to move them forward. They talk about everything they want, they talk about everything that defends them.

As a result of so much over-protection, the son is left without self-esteem. He convinces himself that he is a fool that everything he has and everything he achieves in his life is thanks to his excellent mother, or his great father. In practice, these people who have the "feat of the best parents" as the main feat of their lives… annul their children's personality and trample on their self-esteem.

On the other hand, parents who really love their children do not use them to boast, or to boast ... but rather they work in silence to give them a Strong Self-Esteem that will help them to get ahead in life later on. Parents who really love their children, make them feel that they have their own merits, that they have a life of their own, that they have their own feats ... and not that they are fools, eternal debtors who owe everything to their excellent parents.

-233-

Let's go back to your case ... back to the time you were that age.

At that moment, your own Self-Esteem Map was born, which was the first guide you made to learn how to be someone "valuable" in this world that you were just getting to know.

Your Map of Personal Self-Esteem was similar to that of your parents but it had some differences, because, due to Vanity, we always lied a little.

-234-

Three Maps of Self-Esteem influence you.

1 * The "Map of Social Self-Esteem" (The values, the fundamental feats of your social groups of belonging)

2 * The "Map of your parents' self-esteem" (misrepresented by their own position within that M.A, the feats that parents have revalued and the anti-feats underestimated).

3 * The "Self-esteem Map of your own" (your own values).

... But aren't they the same?

No ... because each person, when it comes to Self-Esteem, "lies a little" in order to feel better.

-235-

When I receive the impact of the great Self-Esteem Map of my society, and I see that I do not have certain feats that, according to this, are fundamental, I tend to value them less so that I can feel a little better and envy less those who do.

At the same time, I tend to overvalue my feats a little so that I can be a little more

proud of what I already am. In this way, I change
the Self-Esteem Map a little and adapt it to my
own situation - I lie a little.

But not in accordance with that, afterwards
I try to influence "my children" so that they also
have a Self-Esteem Map that allows them to value
me more, or to despise me less.

-236-

Now you could try to answer these questions
regarding your parents: What are or what were the
main feats of them?

On what merits do they boast or boast most
often? What were your great glories dreamed of?

And then you could ask yourself ... What
things about them do you think took away their
social prestige? What things do you think
embarrassed them or allowed them to be less proud
of themselves?

-237-

I ask you to make a portrait of the Personal
Map of Self-esteem of each of your parents.

It is an exploration exercise that will help
you a lot to "get to know yourself" because they
influenced you a lot.

What must be done to build the portrait of
the Personal Self-esteem Map of a person ... is
to pay attention especially to their strutting ...
Try to remember what things each of your parents
talked about when they wanted to "show off".

-238-

One of the most important feats on my
mother's Self Esteem Map was being "hardworking,"
being "rebellious," and saying witty phrases.
Whenever she could, she bragged about everything
she achieved with her effort, everything she did
for us, all the things she could buy and could
achieve.

He bragged a lot about that. He pointed to
the walls of our house and said that this was all
for her effort, that she earned it by working.

She was very critical of thieves or the
living who take advantage of the rest and earn
money without working. For her, stealing was one
of the worst anti-feats and she despised anyone
who stole, even if it was bread. She was also very
critical of men who don't work.

In his eyes, not working is a terrible anti-
feat for a man. She also criticized women who do
not work, but not with as much contempt as she
felt for men who do not work. She criticized
priests, criticized the Church, and mocked the
education she had received at a nun school. He
bragged a lot about his own rebellion.

I had a great tendency to reject the codes
of the environments where we moved and to
criticize everyone.

Maybe later I'll tell you a little more ...

-239-

My father bragged a lot about his religious
practices and how good he was, about his physical
appearance -because he went to the gym a lot and

liked the clothes, bracelets and clothes he
bought-, and the family.

He greatly admired social success, he
admired people who are "nice and funny".

For him the great feat was always being
someone "fun". He dressed in exotic colors, and
told many jokes.

It seems to me that he was a believer in
"personal magnetism." I think he saw in some
people the power to draw others around him. He
greatly admired "the sympathetic", the people who
have the gift of being loved or being highly
sought after by "the people".

He was a member of a very important and very
closed religious group. And every week he would
meet with them to chat and pray. He boasted of his
religious practices, of his religious sacrifices,
and criticized superficial people who did not give
God time.

He also bragged about his taste for
decoration, for furniture, for the colors of the
houses, for that kind of thing. He also bragged
about us because he sold us a lot. He was very
proud of his children and cared about us very
much. He also boasted of being a good person.

In his group of friends there was much
respect for economic feats, for the feat of
success, for the feat of social class.

They were looking at things like people's
vocabulary. If you used a certain word, then with
that they identified you as a person with the
anti-feat of the lower social class (a very

important anti-feat for their Social Self-esteem Map).

And, in his circle, there was never talk of "boring" things because being "boring" was one of the most feared and devastating anti-feats.

-240-

Now comes homework: My doctor must find a pen and paper and write an essay about what his parents' Self-Esteem Map looked like.

… I know that I asked for it before and that you are lazy… but it is very important because for a long period of your life they were "your idols".

And therefore, surely they had a very strong impact on your own personality. It is very easy: you should try to remember what kind of things they bragged about, what they talked about when they wanted to show off, what kind of merits the people they admired had ...

The idea is that you write about what they were like in your childhood and adolescence. If you are sufficiently trained in the observation of these things, I encourage you to try to identify, also, what were his main Individualistic Attitudes, and what were his main Political Attitudes.

-241-

When did you feel that you did not meet the expectations that were charged?

When did you feel that you could not achieve the feats that they showed you as essential to reward you with their love and recognition?

When they talked about your life with their
friends… Did they show off some of your merit?

-242-

Your parents influenced you a lot because
they gave you a value system to measure the value
of all people, even your own person.

They also had theirs. And hence they admired
and despised people who are not necessarily the
same as the common people admire and despise.
Because each of them had their own Personal Self-
Esteem Map.

-243-

When the period of "the revolution" arrives,
the child forms his own personality and rebels.

At those moments he understands, for the
first time in his life, that his parents are
normal people. And those feats that in previous
ages he admired, already lose value and do not
seem so great. Then he feels the internal need to
get rid of the idolatry that he professed for so
many years.

The father does not understand what is
happening to his son. He says: What did I do to
make him get so far away from me?

It is that your child needs to build his
personality and to do it the first thing he tries
to do is get rid of the tremendous admiration that
he had before.

And rebelling is his way of fighting that
admiration.

At this point, the child needs to stop seeing them as idols. And, for that, try to contradict them in everything. He looks for new idols and goes out through life to admire a professional of admiration who "works as an idol", seeks refuge in the teenage gang, or tries to be his own idol.

And at that moment the "*Political Attitude*" was born. It is the attempt to change the great Map of Self-Esteem and make one that is more tailored to what "one already is."

-244-

As I was saying ... at that moment in your life you created your own Self-Esteem Map. You dethroned your old idols, and found yourself new ones. And you made your own value system that determined, from then on, who you were going to despise ... who you were going to respect ... And what you had to become to deserve your own applause.

-245-

At that point in your life, then, you made your own Self-Esteem Map.

And you did it by taking three ingredients. On the one hand, the one you already had before which is the one imposed on you by your old idols ... your parents. On the other hand, the one that is part of "your society and your time", the Social Self-Esteem Map that you perceived in the people around you, your brothers, television, books, magazines, advertising, the cinema, what you saw on the street, your friends, your teachers ...

And the third ingredient is your Political
Attitude that improved it a little, carved it a
little ... so that your personal feats are more
valued and your own anti-feats less despised.

-246-

You were influenced by the way you related
to the feats that your parents had always asked
you to give them their applause.

If your relationship was "good" and you were
able to successfully achieve those same feats,
your Self-Esteem Map may not change much compared
to your parents' Self-Esteem Map ... If your
relationship was "bad" and you were hurt a lot,
you got very frustrated ... here it is easier for
you to have needed to rebel more and for that
reason you have embraced values very different
from theirs.

How different was the Personal Self-Esteem
Map you made at that age from your parents'
Personal Self-Esteem Map?

Was it very different? Was it almost the
same?

How different was your own position on that
Self-Esteem Map from your parents' position?

-247-

We should delve a little deeper into that
Map of Social Self-Esteem (M.A.S.) that one comes
across as soon as one stops idolizing his parents
and that he will always be ... because the general
distribution of social prestige in society depends
on him.

The Social Self-Esteem Map is the general
record that comes from the sum of our Self-Esteem
Maps and that distributes prestige in society
according to the feats of each one.

What we call "the values"

-248-

The main subject of study by sociologists
should be precisely this "*Map of Social Self-
Esteem*" that influences so many three fronts:
first, it is the one that pushes people to seek
their feats and thus moves the masses, second, it
determines who the bulk of the people will admire
and whom they will despise ... third, it gives
advertising experts the guidelines they have to
keep in mind to manipulate the masses.

Furthermore, in the face of Social Self-
Esteem Map, people's reaction is not totally
peaceful and meek. It is full of groups that rebel
and try to change it all the time to achieve a new
Social Self-Esteem Map where they are more
recognized and prestigious or less despised.

It is the Political Attitude and it is born
at that age where the boy stops idolizing his
parents and needs to start questioning a little
the values that they impose on him and tries to
"promote" new values that are more friendly to
him.

-249-

Let's keep going…

The Social Self-Esteem Map of the nations
influences their destiny.

Different religions with their different prophets encouraged the worship and contempt for different feats and anti-feats. The religions remarkably influenced the Social Self-Esteem Map and it was this one that determined their destiny.

The different "heroes" endowed with different qualities were a different example of status for their peoples ... different examples that greatly influenced the Social Self-Esteem Map.

Those heroes were praised in their history classes by their teachers, they put them as the name of their avenues, and they put their statues in the squares, and they also put them in their school manuals and on their coins and bills. Those heroes were an "example" that spread, with the passing of the generations, certain values in the towns.

Different Social Self-esteem Map, different destinations for the nations.

-250 -

In the Map of Social Self-esteem, "*stereotyped identities*" are also common.

Positive stereotyped identities are feats that, within themselves, like bags, various feats and configure prestigious stereotypes within popular culture. And negative stereotyped identities are anti-feats that carry other anti-feats within them, generating discredited stereotypes.

They are creations of popular culture, prototype-style characters. If they are valuable,

and you assimilate to one of them, you feel pride
and social prestige. If they are helpless, then
you have shame and dishonor.

Many people give them such importance that
it reduces all their individuality, all the enigma
of their being, all their particular universe, in
one of these stereotypes of the bazaar.

If they are positive stereotyped identities
- identities with feats - you approach them, to
try to feel more pride, and to have more social
prestige. And, if they are negative, you are
walking away, often if you see them very close, it
can be noticed in a constant Individualistic
Attitude trying to get out of it.

-251-

There are also negative stereotyped
identities. They are the ones that have anti-
feats, and if you assume one of them, you lose
social prestige.

For example "a loser". It is a negative
stereotyped identity made with anti-feats of
failure, and defeat in different areas.

All these stereotypes, pre-made characters,
inhabit the Social Self-esteem Map because they
are in popular culture, and when there are people
who wear them - like identities that are bought in
a bazaar - they try to achieve this by increasing
their social prestige. In turn, there are those
who feel trapped by a negative stereotype and use
it to define themselves.

They are a source of prejudice. This is
because they are also used to quickly catalog,
classify and prejudge people.

-252-

What I want you to see is that these
stereotypes and these forces are so determining
that they can shape a whole personality.

You merge with them. You let them fully
absorb you. And finally you define yourself with
one of these molds and say "I am a ..." or say "I
am a ..."

Other times you have a stereotypical
identity on your Personal Self-Esteem Map that
instills fear in you and produces subconscious
emotions that drive behavior away like an inverted
magnet.

-253-

It may be the case for example of the
"fool". Let's call "the fool" a stereotypical
identity built of anti-feats as everyone passes it
by, everyone takes advantage of it, everyone takes
advantage of it and lies to it.

Many live their lives in fear of being taken
for fools.

It is an irrational, strong, subconscious
fear that drives behavior because it is a
stereotypical identity pointed out in his M.A.P.

So, since emotional fear is so powerful,
they spend it doing defensive behaviors that have
the effect of preventing the possibility of
someone taking them for fools. At the end of all,

defensive behaviors cause conflicts with other
people, unnecessary fights, and it turns out that
all these defensive behaviors - which are the
product of fear, an emotional fear of feeling "a
fool" - become a source of harm and obstacles to
their projects and to their success much more
serious than if they were really, ever someone, to
take it for a fool.

It is better to be taken for "fool"
sometimes if the harm is less, than to expose
yourself to the risks of taking disproportionate
aggressive measures just to avoid the risk.
Sometimes it is better to be a fool from time to
time than to "not be fooled" and take
disproportionate preventive measures that, in the
long run, bring much bigger problems.

Many of the worst people I know have this
psychology. They are so afraid of the anti-exploit
of being "taken for fools" that, at the risk of
that, they take aggressive behavior to burst
others and generate all kinds of conflicts and
fights. So, life is full of problems for fear of
that anti-feat and, for the rest of the people,
the best thing is to try to be away from them.

-254-

What are the stereotypical identities of the
Social Self-Esteem Map of your group, of your
society, of your people? What are the ones that
guarantee social prestige? What are the ones that
decrease it?

Have you assumed yourself with a
stereotypical identity?

-255-

We went off topic.

Have you completed the household chores I assigned you?

Let's review ... first of all you must have two essays: one on your father's "Map of Personal Self-Esteem" and one on your mother's "Map of Personal Self-Esteem".

There, with concrete facts and memories of your childhood, it should be clear what things each of your parents boasted about when they wanted to show off.

Then you need to have a third essay ready that talks about the formation of your personality. There it must be developed with many details about what you boasted in those difficult times of your childhood ... and also what wounds you carry from that time.

Was there any feat your parents asked of you that you couldn't achieve? How did you distance yourself from the hero your parents demanded of you?

You must expand at length, paying attention to your great shames and your great glories.

After these three essays ... the third exercise comes that I am going to ask you.

Now you must write the portrait of the " Social Self-Esteem Map" that surrounds you, you must explain about the peculiarities of the of Social Self-Esteem Map of your economic class, your environment, your groups of friends, their time and world. You must develop a treatise on couple relationships today ... about the roles of men and women in your culture, in your environment.

You should try to be critical and point out the good things and the bad things that the Social Self-Esteem Map has in your environment.

-256-

... I found these writings by chance in a wardrobe and returned to it to propose a classification of the "States of Self-Esteem".

Good morning! ... we meet again.

I could tell you that, although it sounds a bit strange and abrupt, I have forgotten you all these months. I found the diary to be broken and messy, and despite that I liked it. And when I read it, it seemed to make sense (so minus the parts I read). I thought it was very good, although it lacks an index so, in the coming days, I will try to put together one to be able to choose the different topics we play.

These are the Three States of Self-Esteem.

-257-

-A- Shattered Self-esteem.

This is the case of the person who does not respect himself, who despises himself and suffers a lot from the intense contempt he has, and may lose the desire for everything, the desire to live, the desire to get up in the morning from bed, the desire to get ready, to bathe, to have fun, to enjoy a movie, a song, the desire for everything.

Many times, in the Shattered Self Esteem, the person defines himself by an anti-feat ... as if it were a black hole that absorbs it. As if the anti-feat had such strength and importance that it becomes its own identity.

An anti-feat has weight in social prestige and that is why the superficial ones call us by the name of our main anti-feat (and they tell us "a loser" or "an old man" or "a fat woman", depending on the anti -feat). But, in the same way, an anti-feat has its effect on a Self-esteem ... and can end up breaking it down.

They may be overwhelmed by defeat, or shame, or see themselves as such, and they name their "anti-feat". For example, if they consider that being over a certain age is an anti-feat, they define themselves with the name of their anti-feat, and say, "I am old"

So a very frequent type of Shattered Self-esteem is for those who have been sucked into an anti-feat. In front of their own eyes, it is their anti-feat that defines them and that is why they are left without Self-Esteem.

Those who have this type of Collapsed Self-Esteem… often incur manipulations for the comfort of others. The woman who has Self-Esteem Collapsed by the anti-feat of not complying with accepted beauty codes says "I am ugly" ... for us to say "no ... you are beautiful" and in that way listen to the comfort that relieves her of the deep pain she has for her anti-feat.

Also who is in this state, sometimes crawls
to achieve feats that puts himself above himself.
For example, he may be a person who, in order to
be accepted by a certain group of people that he
admires or respects, does any number of things in
the style of lowering himself and flattering those
who despise or ignore him.

An example of this would also be a man who
left the couple and who crawls to return to that
woman who abandoned him. He despises himself and
his idea of returning to his partner is above the
respect he has, and then he humiliates himself all
the time with his attempts to regain the love of
the woman who left him.

He who is like this lives inside a dark well
and suffers a lot from this situation and feels
great discouragement and contempt for himself. He
is an easy victim of manipulation ... he is easy
to handle with praise and criticism. And it
depends a lot on the acceptance of other people.

He cannot get angry or defend himself
against offenses or flinch at humiliations because
his self-loathing is so intense that - in a way -
he believes he deserves to be humiliated.

He tries to get out of the pit looking for
impressive triumphs with fantasy plans that are
beyond his own strength. He tries to get the
acceptance of prestigious people, he interprets in
order to obtain the applause of people full of
feats that he admires, crawls, despairs of that
acceptance. He believes that if the prestigious
accept or respect him, he will finally have a
reason to respect himself a little more.

He sacrifices his own personality and his own style to please others, or a particular person he admires. Ask for forgiveness more times than necessary, ask for forgiveness all the time for fear of being disapproved.

It may be a man who, to conform to his partner, changes his clothing style, changes his friends, changes his habits, changes his job, changes his studies, changes his personality, according to what she tells him is better, or what he assumes she will like.

Many times they have a great feat on their horizon: He promises himself to be rewarded with his own acceptance and respect once he reaches that goal.

But in all cases it is not an achievable, practical, concrete goal. It is exaggerated or great things, things out of the ordinary, impressive things that are beyond their own strength. It is such an important triumph that in his eyes he will make up for all his shames and all his defeats that he sees as enormous, because the one who has Collapsed Self-Esteem sees his defeats as enormous and his victories as small.

He is seen left, poorly dressed, sad, hunched, without practical goals, abandoned to the forces of the world. He does not feel like anything, he loses the ability to enjoy the beautiful things in life, he sees everything as black, he cannot have projects, he cannot worry about better and everything does not matter to him. It is like a vegetable that lets life pass and when it wakes up from its lethargy it is due to fantasies of glory or grandiose plans that in the end do not even try to put into practice, or

take the first step to make them concrete, but
then get discouraged and leave everything to half
finished.

-B-Vulnerable Self-esteem.

He is a man who respects himself but his
"self-respect" is too vulnerable to feats and
anti-feats.

Many times he may feel too vulnerable to a
certain person's contempt, or be addicted to that
person's approval ... then there is total
dependence ... that person's approval is needed as
the ultimate feat.

One of the most typical forms of "Vulnerable
Self-Esteem" is what I call "Sustained Self-
Esteem".

And on what is it sustained?

Of feats of course, or rather of a "false
image".

Although such individuals may outwardly
exhibit great self-confidence, the underlying
reality may be just the opposite: the apparent
self-confidence is indicative of their heightened
fear of anti-feats and the fragility of their
self-esteem

They may also try to blame others to protect
their self-image from situations that would
threaten it. They may employ defense mechanisms,
including attempting to lose at games and other
competitions in order to protect their self-image
by publicly dissociating themselves from a need to
win, and asserting an independence from social
acceptance which they may deeply desire. In this

deep fear of being unaccepted by an individual's peers, they make poor life choices by making risky decisions.

Sometimes it is evident that something was wrong or failed, but he cannot see it because if he sees it, he risks destroying his own image and self-respect.

In some cases we find Sustained Self-Esteem in people who have accomplished tremendous feats. They are people who self-admire for the great feats they have, and who, for the same reason, secretly despise almost all people.

He is extremely envious of those who put his superiority at risk. Such a person is all the time counting his feats and desperately hides the anti-feats of his life because he cannot admit them.

When the anti-feats come so strong that you can't deny them or can't look the other way, then it falls directly into the state of Collapsed Self-Esteem but this fall is very painful and feels like falling from a tenth floor.

Many times self-admiration is generated, and this produces a distancing from reality ... crazy. He cannot see his own shortcomings and when the dreaded anti-feats arrive ... then he denies them.

Another thing we see in Sustained Self-Esteem is what I call the immense fear of the "bad decision" anti-feat, the fear of being wrong, the fear of failure. I speak of the extreme panic that an individual can have when making any decision and that this decision will take him one day to look in a mirror and say "all this happened to me was my fault because I was wrong."

It is that the fear of the "bad decision" is not only the heritage of the Sustained Self-Esteem (the boastful people who sustain it about their feats that they talk about incessantly) but also of all types of Vulnerable Self-Esteem. Thus, when someone of this type makes a bad decision, it is most common for them to try to blame everyone around them for not taking responsibility for their own failure.

For example, we are talking about men who blame their women for the state of their lives.

But the immense panic of the "bad decision" is not the exclusive patrimony of the "Sustained Self-Esteem" but of all types of the "Vulnerable Self-Esteem".

The difference is that those who have Sustained Self-Esteem could never admit it because they are horrified by "their own mistake".

What other types of Vulnerable Self-Esteem am I talking about? In other ways, extreme reliance on self-esteem for feats. A good example might be shyness, or invincible fear of ridicule or social error. Shyness is a disease of self-esteem because it is a consequence of the fear of the anti-feat of social failure, of being rejected, of making a fool of oneself, of making a social mistake. There are students who do not dare to sit for an exam even though they have been preparing for a long time to take the exam successfully. And they suffer greatly from the terrible anguish that the risk of being postponed causes them. Some universities - in some terribly competitive countries - have networks so that those who commit suicide after a delay do not hurt others by falling. So you see that different self-esteem is vulnerable to different anti-feats but they share the common trait of extreme vulnerability.

Whoever has Vulnerable Self-Esteem (whether or not it is a case of Sustained Self-Esteem) is a person who has respect for himself, but who lives life as a minefield where inhuman efforts and extravagant pirouettes must be made to dodge anti-feats.

-C- Strong Self-esteem.

People with strong self-esteem have a positive self-image and enough strength so that anti-feats do not subdue their self-esteem. They have less fear of failure. These individuals appear humble, cheerful, and this shows a certain strength not to boast about feats and not to be afraid of anti-feats.

They are capable of fighting with all their might to achieve their goals because, if things go wrong, their self-esteem will not be affected. They can acknowledge their own mistakes precisely because their self-image is strong, and this acknowledgment will not impair or affect their self-image.

They live with less fear of losing social prestige, and with more happiness and general well-being.

Of course, this "strength" of self-esteem is never total, because we all listen to our own lives to respect ourselves. Just as it is not absolute, it can always be improved a little more and every day a self-esteem can become stronger and stronger.

The strength of a self-esteem is recognized in some gestures such as assuming a heavy anti-feat and not hiding it, facing the risk of committing certain anti-feats as a mistake, despising some important feat for your own values or ideals, giving the arm to twist and ask for forgiveness, laugh at yourself.

Whoever has Strong Self-Esteem can sincerely ask for forgiveness. The only one who asks for forgiveness sincerely is the one who does not do it to please the other or does it for fear of being disapproved ... but because he really believes he was wrong. Unlike the cases of Shattered Self-Esteem that ask for forgiveness for any turmoil, that ask for forgiveness for breathing ... in very few occasions whoever has a Strong Self-Esteem asks for forgiveness and does so because they assess that they were seriously wrong.

One of the great virtues of people who have Strong Self-Esteem is that they can make decisions ... and take the risk of being wrong. Also bearers of Strong Self-Esteem have a healthy relationship with their "Success" and can strive to achieve their goals without going crazy and without lowering their arms.

They are kinder, happier, happier, safer, simpler people. They don't brag about their feats all the time and have the gift of being able to laugh at themselves. When they are in a couple they are not very jealous, because if they are disappointed, they do not suffer as if it were death and that immunity makes them enjoy the couple more.

They are capable of listening to the other, of being interested in the other person and of allowing others to be different. They are tolerant of difference and are not overly thirsty for feats. (There is nothing more unpleasant than a person too eager for feats who runs after the feats all the time and who flaunts them all the time).

Furthermore, people who have Strong Self-Esteem have a more sincere and healthier relationship with their peers. When they meet a prestigious person, who enjoys great feats, they do not ask for an autograph or dazzle them… They are capable of having a different opinion from themselves and of defending it. They are not afraid of falling ill or of being despised by others, and they have the inner strength not to be influenced by manipulators.

They are much less envious, less competitive. Their strength is felt in all these behaviors, and since they love what is Strong ... they are often able to awaken more often the feelings of Admiration.

These people also fight for their goals and also achieve feats ... The strength of their self-esteem lies in the freedom they have to - sometimes - put that aside and follow their own thoughts or ideals. They are able to forgive, they are able to admit a mistake, they are able to change their minds in an argument. They are able to put themselves in the other's place and empathize with the other's shame.

They are happy, simple, enthusiastic people and they can look at those whom they have great anti-feats, as if they were an equal, as if they

were a brother. They are able to tear down the
walls of their own pride and imagine how they
would feel if they had the anti-feats of their
neighbor and to feel how their neighbor feels, to
feel how their neighbor looks at the world.

The ability to laugh at their own mistakes
allows them the difficult exercise of making
decisions. And, for this reason, they assume their
responsibility in the state of their lives and
with perseverance and will direct it towards their
greatest projects and their greatest goals

People who have a "Strong Self-Esteem" enjoy
their time, they don't brag about their feats all
the time. They are able to run with all their
might, even in those races where they know they
can finish last. They are capable of making
decisions, even assuming the risk that they are
wrong. They are able to ask for forgiveness and to
make their own mistakes.

People who have Strong Self-Esteem generate
an independent, autonomous personality. They can
laugh at themselves ... You can admit your anti-
feats naturally, you may not flaunt your feats. It
is noticed even in the body posture, its security
... It is still noticed in their gestures and
their way of speaking that they do not beg for
approval and that they are indifferent to the
opinion of the rest.

All those things are achieved by people who
have Strong Self-Esteem and they are also people
who, above all, enjoy life more.

I think it is very difficult today to
achieve Strong Self-Esteem because we are in a
world of deformed mirrors where we all want to be

what we are not, for all these things that we talk
about elsewhere. We are too hard to judge errors:
ours and others'. And what is good we see as small
and unimportant, on the other hand, what is bad we
make giant, we exaggerate until our vision is
clouded and it prevents us from seeing everything
else.

But there are still people with strong self-
esteem and they are the best. The least
competitive, the most cheerful. From time to time,
we meet one of these simple, simple, happy people,
who have Strong Self-Esteem and who can connect
much better with our personal shames and
understand them. They are people who can connect
with our exploits and celebrate them without
feeling envy. They are much happier and they
spread part of this happiness around them because
they are happier with their achievements - and if
they are small they do not detract from them and
if they are large they do not show them.

Equally, Strong Self-Esteem is one thing and
Invincible Self-Esteem is another. Strong Self-
Esteem can be real and can be found both in people
who have achieved impressive feats and have great
social prestige, as in others who have a simpler
life but are very safe. On the other hand,
Invincible Self-Esteem seems to me to be a myth, a
legend ... because we can all fall into the well
sometime, we are all exposed to our Self-Esteem
being demolished. And it is not so serious because
you can always get out of that situation the same.
Discouragement can always be overcome and it is
even possible to take advantage of it to reach new
horizons.

9 798650 156079